Newcomer's S E R I E S

365 TIPS
FOR NEWCOMERS
Your First Year
in Canada

365 TIPS FOR NEWCOMERS
Your First Year in Canada

Nick Noorani
Best-selling author
"Arrival Survival Canada"

Self-Counsel Press
(a division of)
International Self-Counsel Press Ltd.
Canada   USA

Self-Counsel Press acknowledges the financial support of the Government of Canada through the Canada Book Fund for our publishing activities.

First edition: 2014

Library and Archives Canada Cataloguing in Publication

Noorani, Naeem, 1957–, author
    365 tips for newcomers : your first year in Canada / Nick Noorani.

(Self-Counsel newcomers series)
Issued in print and electronic formats.
ISBN 978-1-77040-210-2 (pbk.).—ISBN 978-1-77040-960-6 (epub).—ISBN 978-1-77040-961-3 (kindle)

    1. Immigrants—Canada—Handbooks, manuals, etc. 2. Canada—Emigration and immigration. I. Title. II. Title: Three hundred sixty five tips for newcomers. III. Series: Self-Counsel newcomers series

JV7220.N66 2014   325.71   C2014-905609-5

Foreword written by Dr. Peter Legge, OBC, LL.D (Hon), D. Tech, used with permission.

Every effort has been made to obtain permission for quoted material where necessary. If there is an omission or error, the author and publisher would be grateful to be so informed.

Self-Counsel Press
(a division of)
International Self-Counsel Press Ltd.

Bellingham, WA   North Vancouver, BC
USA   Canada

Contents

Notice to Readers

Laws are constantly changing. Every effort is made to keep this publication as current as possible. However, the author, the publisher, and the vendor of this book make no representations or warranties regarding the outcome or the use to which the information in this book is put and are not assuming any liability for any claims, losses, or damages arising out of the use of this book. The reader should not rely on the author or the publisher of this book for any professional advice. Please be sure that you have the most recent edition.

Dedication

This book is for the millions of immigrants the world over. The everyday people who leave everything they have in search of a dream. I feel your pain and your challenges and want you to soar! This book contains tips and quotes that will inspire you and keep you focused on self-improvement as a way to success.

Dedicated to my late father, Hafeez "Happy" Noorani, one of the most inspirational humans I have had the privilege of knowing; and to my late mother, Zubeida "Zubi" Noorani, for her dedication to our becoming good humans.

This book is also dedicated to the many who motivate me on an ongoing basis (they know who they are!) and a few people I interact with on a more frequent basis.

To "JK," thank you for what you do for immigrants and Canada!

To my dear friend, and mentor, Praveen Varshney; and fellow author, publisher, and entrepreneur, Peter Legge.

To David Frattini, friend and business partner: Thank you for believing in me and for your friendship.

Lastly, to my wife, Sabrina, for her continuous encouragement (and redoing drafts of my books!) and my children Michelle and Daanish.

Foreword

One of the things I admire about Nick Noorani is his commitment and passion to welcoming new immigrants to Canada.

When my parents Win and Bernie Legge made a life-changing decision to emigrate from London, England, some 60 years ago, even though they had assisted passage, there wasn't very much help or guidance upon their arrival to New Westminster, British Columbia.

Some 65 years ago, setting sail from Southampton were hundreds, perhaps even thousands of immigrants from the British Isles and Europe. Optimistic new entrepreneurs and immigrants got off their ships at Pier 22 in Halifax, looking for a new life somewhere in this great country of Canada. My father came to the "Royal City" of New Westminster, and he got off a bus at the Greyhound bus depot, which is now the Royal Towers Hotel opposite the New

Westminster City Hall. My dad had no road map, no instructions, and no guidance, just his good common sense. He picked blueberries on a Fraser Valley farm, washed dishes in a Kingsway diner, did whatever he could to earn a few dollars to survive in this new country as he continued looking for a full-time position to support his wife and his one son ... me.

Almost a year went by with little to no success. Discouraged, despondent, and almost beat, he took a job in Kitimat, BC, on a six-month contract at Alcan, just to make enough money so he could sail back home to England. The day before he was to leave for Kitimat, he heard of an inside sales job at a well-established company in New Westminster — Gilley Brothers — and was hired on the spot, so Kitimat never happened. Our home was to be in New Westminster.

Sixty-five years ago, new immigrants were not provided with guidance books, or government liaison organizations to assist them. Some barely spoke any English; fortunately we did not have that problem.

Nick Noorani has spent a lifetime with a deep and passionate interest in helping immigrants get settled in Canada. His book, *365 Tips for Newcomers: Your First Year in Canada* is a *must read* for all new Canadians. The advice and counsel are essential to integrating into Canadian culture as quickly as possible. If Canada is your new home, this should be the first book you read. I wish it was available when we arrived here.

Dr. Peter Legge, OBC, LL.D. (Hon), D. Tech.
Chairman/CEO/Publisher
Canada Wide Media Limited

Introduction

What keeps the earth turning are the thousands of immigrants walking to new destinations every day, pushing the planet around and around with their millions of footsteps.

— Anonymous

Immigrants often ask me where I get my energy and inspiration. The fact is my life's goal to motivate others comes from my late father, Hafeez Noorani. He had the ability to look at the good and the opportunity in most every situation. Not surprisingly, Dad was also nicknamed "Happy"! Now when I ask my two-year-old granddaughter, "Laila, how are you?" she smiles and says, "Happy"! Life comes full circle!

Here's a fact: The first year in any new country is the most difficult. Lack of friends, family, the support network one was used to, struggling to find a job, and becoming accustomed to a new and often very different culture present some of the greatest challenges of your life. It is therefore not surprising that a number of immigrants return home during that critical first year.

How do you avoid becoming another statistic? It's about moving out of your comfort zone and accepting that change is about more than physically moving to a different country; it's about finding greater opportunities and building a better future for yourself and your family.

How do you cope with such a transition? How do you keep yourself from becoming that dreaded statistic of failure? Don't spend a lot of time on Facebook, emailing, chatting, and Skyping friends and relatives back home. Stop watching movies and programs only in your language. You'll not only make yourself constantly homesick but you're setting yourself up to fail if you allow nostalgia to weaken your resolve to succeed in your new country!

Fear kills happiness. It breeds uncertainty, doubt, and worry. Most fears are unfounded, but we are instinctively afraid of the unknown, which in turn fuels our fear even more. Why? Sometimes, we are our own worst enemy. We obsess about failure and overthink the slightest setback. Our longing for the familiarity of the past and a comfortable routine defeat our initiative. Fight these negative influences with constructive distractions. Try new things, and step outside your door. Volunteer with local organizations to get a feel for your new community. Attend classes, refine your English skills, take up a sport, and join a gym. There are so many wonderful things to learn about your new country. Consider it a vacation with no time limit!

I wanted to write a book for the first year filled with sayings from several wise people and how I see these quotes as being relevant to an immigrant's journey. They are guidelines from others who have walked a similar path to success so learn from these words of wisdom. Several immigrants who read the initial manuscript asked me to also write my own thoughts and I have put in a few as well. For the past 16 years I have worked hard for immigrants to strengthen themselves. I believe this book will help. Believe in the power of positive affirmations. Read a quote every day to fuel the passion!

Network, vocalize, and create a circle of influential people that will empower you to greater achievements. Review, reinvent, recharge, and *succeed*!

Canada Is Different

How to define Canada? It's not always easy to pinpoint exactly what being Canadian means. Often, Canada is compared to its neighbour to the south. Yes, we share a border with Americans, but we are not really the same. Many immigrants who come to Canada for the first time have most of their impressions based on what they see in the movies, but Hollywood is in the United States, not Canada. While the two countries have similarities, there is something unique about Canada as a country and a people, compared not only to the United States, but also to other countries around the world.

Half of my siblings live in the United States, and I visited them several times before I migrated to Canada. After I arrived in Canada, I was expecting a similar atmosphere, but I was truly struck by how different Canadians are. Oh yes, the stereotype of the Canadian being too "nice" is true!

I remember driving on Georgia Street in Vancouver for the first time (this was before GPS) and we were hopelessly inept at understanding a map. We paused to ask a cyclist for directions and he said, "No problem, just follow me." We followed him to the location in the opposite direction to where he was going! This is one of so many stories I have experienced and heard from immigrants. What makes Canada different? I believe it is the people.

Sure, there are other things that seem quite "Canadian." We do love our Tim Hortons coffee. We have access to public health care. We enjoy the vast outdoors, watch hockey, celebrate multiculturalism, and do get into the habit of saying "eh," but the true identity of Canada is in Canadians themselves.

Having lived and worked in four countries, I am constantly amazed at the Canadian heart and often say it is as big as the very size of this great country! Sure, you will meet the occasional nasty person who may make you question what I am saying, but that oddball is a small percentage among Canadians. Canadians are by and large very kind and embracing of immigrants.

Like any other country, Canada has had a controversial history with examples of intolerance and discrimination, from the treatment of the Chinese rail workers brought in to build the Trans-Canada Railway to the treatment of its Aboriginal Peoples, and some forms of discrimination still exist. However, it's a different country today, where you can find immigrants at the highest levels of government and industry. The last two of three Governor Generals of Canada were, in fact, immigrants! They do not reach such heights because they are or are not immigrants, but because they are good at what they do and were accepted in this great country as equals. With the right attitude, anyone can be accepted and succeed in Canada!

Tip 1

Cause change and lead; accept change and survive; resist change and die.

— Ray Norda, businessperson

Your decision to move to a foreign country brought change to your life. Now you must do whatever is necessary to make it fruitful.

Tip 2

It is better to risk starving to death than surrender. If you give up on your dreams, what's left?

— Jim Carrey, actor, comedian, and producer

Don't give up your dreams in the face of adversities. You did not come to this foreign country to lead an ordinary life. Those who made it to the top toiled for hours to become what they are today.

Tip 3

The potter forms what he pleases with soft clay, so a man accomplishes his works by his own act.

— Hitopadesha, Sanskrit fables

Just as the potter gives shape to the soft clay and forms an earthen pot, we also form our own destiny through our thoughts and actions.

Tip 4

Take advantage of every opportunity to practice your communication skills so that when important occasions arise, you will have the gift, the style, the sharpness, the clarity, and the emotions to affect other people.

— Jim Rohn, entrepreneur, author, and motivational speaker

Communication skills are critical for immigrants. Read, write, and speak in English or French as much as possible to get on par with natives.

Tip 5

Language is the road map of a culture. It tells you where its people come from and where they are going.

— Rita Mae Brown, author

Learning a new language will help you to understand the culture, history, and traditions of the host country. This is very helpful to relate to people and strike up a conversation. I learned how to say "Hello" to my audiences in 17 different languages! What a difference it makes to them!

Tip 6

Behold the turtle. It makes progress only when it sticks its neck out.

— James Bryant Conant

Immigrants take the biggest risk by leaving all that they know in their home countries, and migrate to the unknown on the basis of their own self confidence and abilities, but after migrating they want to play safe! You will have to continue to take risks to succeed. Risks could be in the form of learning new skills, trusting your intuition, acting on an alternate plan, or starting your own business.

Tip 7

You have brains in your head. You have feet in your shoes. You can steer yourself any direction you choose. You're on your own. And you know what you know. And YOU are the one who'll decide where to go ...

— Dr. Seuss, author and cartoonist
Oh, The Places You'll Go

Set your goal and direct your hard work and intelligence towards it.

Tip 8

If you have built castles in the air, your work need not be lost; that is where they should be. Now put the foundations under them.

— Henry *Walden* David Thoreau, author and philosopher

Don't let your dream remain a dream. Start with the foundation of focus, hard work, and dedicated efforts to convert those dreams into reality.

Tip 9

Twenty years from now you will be more disappointed by the things that you didn't do than by the ones you did do. So throw off the bowlines. Sail away from the safe harbor. Catch the trade winds in your sails. Explore. Dream. Discover.

— Mark Twain, author

The greatest regret in life is looking back and wishing you had followed your dreams. Don't let fear rob you of your goals.

Tip 10

The intensity of the pain depends on the degree of resistance to the present moment ...

— Eckhart Tolle, author and public speaker

When you embrace change, much of the pain of moving out of your comfort zone will either disappear or make it easier for you to handle.

Tip 11

The immigrant who succeeds is the one who understands that this is a different country and things are done differently here from back "home" and adapts to it.

— Nick (Naeem) Noorani, immigrant champion, author, and motivational speaker

Tip 12

You may never know what results come from your action. But if you do nothing, there will be no result.

— Mahatma Gandhi, inspired movements for civil rights and freedoms across the world

Inaction means certain failure, so why not take your chances!

Tip 13

Action may not always bring happiness; but there is no happiness without action.

— Benjamin Disraeli, former British Prime Minister

If you do not act on your dreams, you will never be happy.

Tip 14

Without a sense of urgency, desire loses its value.

— Jim Rohn, entrepreneur, author, and motivational speaker

Plan how are you going to reach your goals and put that plan into action. The more you delay, the more difficult it will become. Start immediately and stay determined.

Tip 15

Success comes from taking the initiative and following up ... persisting ... eloquently expressing the depth of your love. What simple action could you take today to produce a new momentum toward success in your life?

— Tony Robbins, performance coach, author, motivational speaker, and actor

Success means taking that first step toward your dream and following each step with another. This gives you the momentum to keep going.

Tip 16

Let's make a dent in the universe.

— Steve Jobs, entrepreneur, marketer, and inventor

We all have the ability and strength inside us to make an impression on the world. It is just a matter of how much effort you make.

Tip 17

Time is neutral and does not change things. With courage and initiative, leaders change things.

— Jesse Jackson, Baptist minister and activist

You are wrong in thinking that someday things will magically change to create a brighter future. It is your determination and efforts that will bring about that change.

Tip 18

The vision must be followed by the venture. It is not enough to stare up the steps — we must step up the stairs.

— Vance Havner, minister and author

To realize your vision, you need to translate it into an action plan and start putting it into practice.

Tip 19

Those who wait until all the lights are on green before starting will never leave home.

— Zig Ziglar, author, salesman, and motivational speaker

If you keep waiting for all things to become perfect before you act, then that will never happen. You have to start now whatever be the situation.

 Tip 20

Whenever you see a successful business, someone once made a courageous decision.

— Peter F. Drucker, author, professor, and management consultant

Don't hesitate to make tough decisions.

Tip 21

Have the end in mind and every day make sure you are working towards it.

— Ryan Allis, entrepreneur

Stay focused on your ultimate goal and make each day count as you progress toward it.

Tip 22

One day your life will flash before your eyes. Make sure it is worth watching.

— Author unknown

Make your life a success story that is valuable to listen to and discuss in later years.

Tip 23

I think that anybody that smiles automatically looks better.

— Diane Lane, actress

A smile not only enhances your physical appearance but also adds to your overall personality. People are more inclined to interact with people who smile and seem friendly.

Tip 24

Once you agree upon the price you and your family must pay for success, it enables you to ignore the minor hurts, the opponent's pressure, and the temporary failures.

— Vince Lombardi, football player, coach, and executive

Talk to your family and explain how important your dreams are. They will understand. Mutually prioritize what you will trade off to achieve the success. Once you do that, you will realize your family is your greatest strength that will support your dreams in the face of challenges.

Tip 25

But today, our very survival depends on our ability to stay awake, to adjust to new ideas, to remain vigilant and to face the challenge of change.

— Martin Luther King, Jr., pastor, activist, humanitarian, and leader of the African-American Civil Rights Movement

Stay current with what's happening in the world around you. Be aware of new ideas and emerging demands to create opportunities for growth.

Tip 26

Before you start some work, always ask yourself three questions — Why am I doing it, what the results might be and will I be successful? Only when you think deeply and find satisfactory answers to these questions, go ahead.

— Chanakya, teacher, philosopher, and royal advisor

Closely analyze all your actions to confirm they contribute to the long-term goal.

Tip 27

There are no constraints on the human mind, no walls around the human spirit, no barriers to our progress except those we ourselves erect.

— Ronald Reagan,
former President of the United States

As the wise Yoda from *Star Wars* said, "Do. Or do not. There is no try." (Sorry, I had to sneak this one in!)

Tip 28

In the dim background of mind we know what we ought to be doing but somehow we cannot start.

— William James, philosopher,
psychologist, and physician

It's not enough to always think about your dreams and desires for success. What's stopping you from moving forward?

Tip 29

Do not wait until the conditions are perfect to begin. Beginning makes the conditions perfect.

— Alan Cohen, author

No "perfect time" is without the risks! Start acting on your dreams and your actions will change the environment in your favor.

Tip 30

There are two mistakes one can make along the road to truth ... not going all the way, and not starting.

— Buddha

Quitting halfway and never starting are the greatest mistakes people make.

Tip 31

The graveyard is the richest place on earth, because it is here that you will find all the hopes and dreams that were never fulfilled, the books that were never written, the songs that were never sung, the inventions that were never shared, the cures that were never discovered, all because someone was too afraid to take that first step, keep with the problem, or determined to carry out their dream.

— Les Brown, motivational speaker,
former politician, author, and radio DJ

My friend and mentor from early days used to say it's the things you don't do that you regret. I therefore had no problem with taking risks.

Tip 32

It is never too late to be what you might have been.

— George Eliot, author

We often make excuses for not working on our dreams. Get rid of those excuses and start now!

Tip 33

I am not afraid of storms for I am learning how to sail my ship.

— Louisa May Alcott, author

Don't let fear of the unknown hinder your goals.

Tip 34

The way to get started is to quit talking and begin doing.

— Walt Disney, entrepreneur, cartoonist,
filmmaker, philanthropist

Talk accomplishes only so much. Actions transform dreams into reality.

Tip 35

It's your place in the world; it's your life. Go on and do all you can with it, and make it the life you want to live.

— Dr. Mae Jemison, physician and NASA astronaut

Utilize all your potential, abilities, and resources to create a better quality of life for yourself and your family.

Tip 36

The best way to predict your future is to create it.

— Abraham Lincoln, lawyer and former President of the United States

You are completely in charge of your future.

Tip 37

Other people's opinion of you does not have to become your reality.

— Les Brown, motivational speaker, former politician, author, and radio DJ

Quitters will tell you that it is impossible to realize your dreams in a new country. Pay no attention to such negative thinking.

Tip 38

If you're always strict with yourself, life gets miserable. And we're supposed to enjoy life.

— Mía Maestro, actress

Don't always be tough on yourself. Take time off to appreciate the beauty of your new country. Enjoy the country where you dreamed of living.

Tip 39

If you never try, you'll never know what you are capable of.

— John Barrow, politician

The best test of your abilities is to navigate through challenging situations. You will be amazed by what you discover about yourself.

What to Know before You Go

Why do some immigrants fail and some succeed? One of the biggest factors that determines an immigrant's chance for success or failure in Canada today is his or her research and preparation — or lack thereof.

It always amazes me when I hear of how some people can uproot their lives and families and travel around the world to a land that is vastly different from what they were accustomed to, without doing substantial homework.

When I came to Canada from Dubai, the Internet was in its infancy and not as much information was available as there is today. Even at that time, I spent hours on forums getting information on Canada, its people, and workplace culture. Yet, I tripped up on two very important aspects.

My first mistake was assuming. With my background in advertising, I simply expected Vancouver, as a major Canadian city, to have a healthy and robust advertising industry. Not so! Most advertising in the late 1990s was done in Toronto and the Vancouver offices were mainly liaison offices. Never assume! Ask.

Like most immigrants, I chose Vancouver because I knew someone who was already living there; in this case my brother, who had migrated two years before me. While having such connections is important, it shouldn't be the sole determinant of where you choose to settle. Canada is a vast country, with very diverse regions and economies, and if I knew then what I know now, I probably would have chosen to be in a location where my profession was more prolific.

The second mistake was so silly that I am almost embarrassed to admit it. We brought a huge container from Dubai laden with furniture, clothes, and electronics. I completely forgot that the North American voltage is 120, not 240! I had three TVs, VCRs, hair dryers, cookers, etc., and all were useless in Canada, except for my big screen TV and stereo system, which had dual voltage.

Another thing I wish I had known before coming to Canada was the difference in the English language. To many immigrants who come from Asia, the Middle East, Africa, and Latin American countries, the English they learned back home is much different than the version spoken in Canada. I was educated in a private school, went to an upscale university, and spoke English as my first language. Yet the English I speak today is dramatically different from what I spoke back home.

Let's talk accents. I didn't have one before I came to Canada because everyone around me spoke just like me! Now I am in this new country with many of its inhabitants have distinct accents. Here's a tip: Speak slowly and watch the the news on CBC. Now try imitating the newscaster. It takes some time, but you will eventually learn how to speak Canadian.

Lastly, you must learn corporate English, both written and verbal. There are plenty of books on this subject, so do get some from your library. Email etiquette is increasingly becoming an area where immigrants trip themselves up, so pay attention to how you communicate in person and online.

Tip 40

The elevator to success is out of order. You'll have to use the stairs ... one step at a time.

— Joe Girard, salesperson and public speaker

Success is not achieved in a day to two. It requires a precisely detailed action plan and determination to follow each item on the plan. Read, research, and act!

Tip 41

Every immigrant who comes here should be required within five years to learn English or leave the country.

— Theodore Roosevelt, former president of the United States, author

Learning a new language is a difficulty encountered by most immigrants but at the same time it is also a very critical element to their success. Employers are reluctant to hire immigrants with poor language and soft skills. Research also points to increased chances of getting a suitable job if you have an ability to speak English.

Tip 42

Whatever country you go to, you need to definitely follow the rules. So I believe it's very important for people, wherever they go, any immigrant should know or should try to learn something about the culture.

— David Ortiz, professional baseball player

It is important to know about the heritage and norms of the host country's culture. This goes a long way to start conversations and avoid embarrassing situations. Embracing your new country, its history, and its traditions will make you feel like you belong.

Tip 43

Go confidently in the direction of your dreams. Live the life you've imagined.

— Henry David Thoreau, author and philosopher

When you took the decision to immigrate, you had big dreams of success glittering in your eyes. Don't let anything or anyone destroy those dreams. Be confident of your abilities and your decision. Walk towards your dream with unwavering commitment and your dreams are sure to come true.

Tip 44

If you do not have language skills on par with the native population, all your technical skills and experience is like the world's biggest diamond, in a cave at the bottom of the ocean — priceless and worthless!

— Nick (Naeem) Noorani, immigrant champion, author, and motivational speaker

Only when you are able to speak and communicate your knowledge in a language that employers understand will you be able to showcase your vast technical skills and years of experience. Until then, they will remain uncovered. Research studies indicate that language skills have a large impact on the ability of immigrants to find high-paying jobs in their chosen fields.

Tip 45

The man who removes a mountain begins by carrying away small stones.

— Confucius

All great things are achieved by taking small steps.

Tip 46

If not us, who? If not now, when?

— Hillel the Elder, religious leader

Don't delay starting your journey to success. Whatever the circumstances are, you should plan and act rather than wait for things to change on their own. Remember, there will never be the "perfect" time.

Tip 47

The typical immigrant journey comprises three parts: getting the first job, retaining it, and growing in that job. Too many immigrants focus on one or two parts and need to work on all three in order to have an ideal outcome.

— Nick (Naeem) Noorani, immigrant champion, author, and motivational speaker

Tip 48

The journey of a thousand miles begins with one step.

— Lao Tzu, philosopher and poet

The journey to success is a long one and the truth is, you will encounter obstacles along the way. Taking the first step is the most difficult and the most important.

Tip 49

Either you run the day or the day runs you.

— Jim Rohn, entrepreneur, author, and motivational speaker

Don't be a slave to time and circumstances. Take control of your life and create your own path.

Tip 50

Plan B is what happens when Plan A doesn't work. Unfortunately, Plan A has a habit of not always working. To make matters worse, most immigrants have no plan at all!

— Nick (Naeem) Noorani, immigrant champion, author, and motivational speaker

Tip 51

Don't wait for something big to occur. Start where you are, with what you have, and that will always lead you into something greater.

— Mary Manin Morrissey, life coach, motivational speaker, and author

You can't regain time lost if you wait for that perfect day to start. Begin with whatever resources you have.

Tip 52

A good plan implemented today is better than a perfect plan implemented tomorrow.

— George Patton, army general

Don't spend too much time perfecting your plan. Get into action. There will be many things you discover on the way.

Tip 53

The best thing about the future is that it comes one day at a time.

— Abraham Lincoln, former president of the United States

Take action every day to make progress every day.

Tip 54

In order to succeed, your desire for success should be greater than your fear of failure.

— Bill Cosby, actor, comedian, author, and activist

Passion to achieve your dream should be stronger than your fear of failure. Only then will you move forward.

Tip 55

The secret of getting ahead is getting started. The secret of getting started is breaking your complex, overwhelming tasks into small, manageable tasks, and then starting on the first one.

— Mark Twain, author and humorist

To reach your goal you must first prepare an action plan. Break the journey into milestones and focus on the first milestone.

Tip 56

"Someday" doesn't exist, never has, and never will. There is no "someday." There's only today. When tomorrow comes, it will be another today; so will the next day. They all will. There is never anything but today.

— Jeff Olson, entrepreneur and author

Don't keep postponing things to tomorrow. Act today.

Tip 57

You don't have to be great to get started, but you have to get started to be great.

— Les Brown, motivational speaker,
former politician, author, and radio DJ

Success necessitates action. Without action, you won't realize anything.

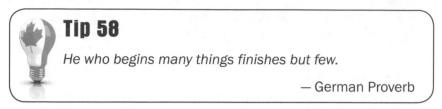

Tip 58

He who begins many things finishes but few.

— German Proverb

Pursue your goals without distractions.

Tip 59

Don't be afraid to give up the good to go for the great.

— John D. Rockefeller, entrepreneur and philanthropist

Do not settle for second best. Keep your eyes focused on your dreams and go for gold!

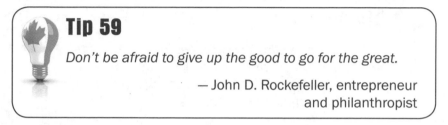

Tip 60

Success demands singleness of purpose.

— Vince Lombardi, football player, coach, and executive

Dedicate all your resources — time, effort, and money — to pursue one goal.

Tip 61

Focus: Follow One Course Until Successful

— Robert Kiyosaki, entrepreneur, author, motivational speaker, and financial commentator

Too many people get distracted by shiny baubles. Keep focused and success will follow.

Tip 62

The way I see it, if you want the rainbow, you gotta put up with the rain.

— Dolly Parton, singer-songwriter, actress, author, and philanthropist

To get the desired results, you have to face challenges.

Tip 63

The beginning is the most important part of the work.

— Plato, philosopher and mathematician

Plan and act. Conquer your fears and take that first step.

Tip 64

Stop the habit of wishful thinking and start the habit of thoughtful wishes.

— Mary Martin, actress and singer

You have a dream, but only thinking about your dream without acting on it accomplishes nothing. Success is achieved when you put your thoughts into action.

Tip 65

I hated every minute of training, but I said, "Don't quit. Suffer now and live the rest of your life as a champion."

— Muhammad Ali, former professional boxer

Most times in life, we have to get the really hard grind out of the way. After that it gets easier.

Tip 66

Every great story on the planet happened when someone decided not to give up, but kept going no matter what.

— Spryte Loriano, author

Behind all success stories there are years of struggle and hard work to overcome challenges. The decision to not quit but continue the pursuit of success has made many leaders.

Tip 67

When everything seems to be going against you, remember that the airplane takes off against the wind, not with it.

— Henry Ford, entrepreneur

Use adversity to fuel your determination to succeed even more.

Tip 68

It does not matter how slowly you go as long as you do not stop.

— Confucius

Small steps are still steady progress toward your goal.

Tip 69

Few things in the world are more powerful than a positive push. A smile. A world of optimism and hope. And you can do it when things are tough.

— Richard M. DeVos, entrepreneur

A positive attitude is the key to overcoming challenges. Focus on solving problems and achieving your goal rather than being overwhelmed by challenges.

Tip 70

Striving for success without hard work is like trying to harvest where you haven't planted.

— David Bly

Success comes only after you have planted the seeds through effort and hard work.

Tip 71

You are never given a wish without also being given the power to make it come true. You may have to work for it, however.

— Richard Bach, author

You have the abilities and power to achieve your goal. Make your vision a reality through action instead of wishing.

Tip 72

Careers, like rockets, don't always take off on schedule. The key is to keep working the engines.

— Gary Sinise, actor, director, and musician

Though you might not yet have achieved your goal, continue working toward it.

Tip 73

The heights by great men reached and kept were not attained by sudden flight, but they, while their companions slept, were toiling upward in the night.

— Henry Wadsworth Longfellow, poet

Success demands long hours of hard work and commitment while others are having fun.

Have Realistic Expectations

Many immigrants migrate at the peak of their careers and, understandably, want to pick up where they left off when they move to Canada. Unfortunately, that scenario is very rare. Most immigrants have to start at the bottom and work their way up. Many seem quite surprised and upset by this. You may have arrived here with stars in your eyes and excitement in your heart; however, your first year in Canada will be the hardest. You'll likely be friendless, jobless, and a little bit homesick, for a while — no wonder a percentage of immigrants return home in the first year (www.statcan. gc.ca/daily-quotidien/060301/dq060301b-eng.htm).

The reality is that it takes some time to adjust to a new country. Things are different here, after all. Fortunately, after a few months in Canada, most newcomers start to understand this fact. I quickly realized it, too. I came to Canada with 23 years of experience in advertising and after hearing the common response from employers, "Sorry, but you have no Canadian experience," I decided to look at a Plan B career option and soon landed a job in advertising sales at a small publishing company. Was it at the level I was at in Dubai? No. But that job created the foundation for me launching my own magazine five years later!

Here's the point: It took me 23 years to reach where I was in the advertising industry in my home country, so I cannot realistically expect I will instantly be at the same point in a new country. That just doesn't make sense. You have to build up experience and connections in Canada before your worth is recognized. Canada needs time to get to know you.

Have realistic expectations when you come to Canada. Does that mean you should give up and accept defeat? No. I still believe you should aim for the sky. It just might take some time, hard work, and a little luck to reach that high.

Tip 74

The only thing worse than being blind is having sight but no vision.

— Helen Keller, author, political activist, and lecturer

Create a vision of where you want to see yourself in this new country; for example, ten years from now. You have boarded this flight to reach somewhere and not "anywhere." Rather than being driven by circumstances you should take the baton in your hand and propel your life in the new land towards that ultimate goal: A vision of being a successful entrepreneur, educator, IT professional, business executive, or anything else.

Tip 75

I don't sell fish. I help immigrants fish so they never go hungry!

— Nick (Naeem) Noorani, immigrant champion, author, and motivational speaker

I won't give you a job but as someone who has met and advised several immigrants on how to succeed, I know what you need. You need a plan and the ability to move out of your comfort zones. This knowledge will never let you be jobless.

Tip 76

Some men look at things the way they are and ask why? I dream of things that are not and ask why not?

— George Bernard Shaw, playwright, critic, and political activist

This is especially true when you consider the world's greatest immigrant entrepreneurs. How were they able to come up with ideas that no one else could?

 **Tip 77**

Goals allow you to control the direction of change in your favor.

— Brian Tracy, entrepreneur, public speaker, author, and personal and professional development trainer

It is helpful to set specific time-bound goals for yourself. This will ensure that your energy, efforts, resources, and time stay focused on the right track.

Tip 78

You have to be able to risk your identity for a bigger future than the present you are living.

— Fernando Flores, engineer, entrepreneur, and politician

Sometimes you have to accept a job that does not match your current technical competence but remember all this is for a better and more prosperous future.

Tip 79

The notion is that having the soft skills doesn't guarantee you the job, but not having them puts you at real risk of not even getting an offer.

— David Wilson, football player

To get that dream job you require both "soft skills" as well as "technical skills." Lack of even one of them puts you at a disadvantage.

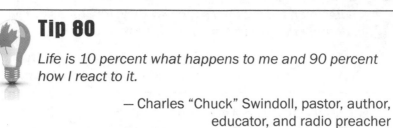

Tip 80

Life is 10 percent what happens to me and 90 percent how I react to it.

— Charles "Chuck" Swindoll, pastor, author, educator, and radio preacher

Our life is the outcome of our responses to different situations and people. I have very little control over what happens to me. I have complete control over how I react to what is happening to me.

Tip 81

There is only one thing that makes a dream impossible to achieve: the fear of failure.

— Paulo Coelho, lyricist and novelist

Many immigrants who were denied a job by local employers went on to start their own ventures and are now successful entrepreneurs. Then there were others who, on not achieving their dream job, continued in a survival job or went back to their home country. What you make of your life is a matter of how you handle life's obstacles.

Tip 82

What you do today can improve all your tomorrows.

— Ralph Marston, Jr., author

You will gain success for the efforts that you will put in today. That is the only way to secure a better future for you and your next generations.

Tip 83

Setting goals is the first step in turning the invisible into the visible.

— Tony Robbins, performance coach, author, motivational speaker, and actor

Without specific time-bound goals we will run a race without a finishing line!

Tip 84

Never be afraid to make a mistake. Learnings come through embracing failure. Just don't make the same mistakes again!

— Nick (Naeem) Noorani, immigrant champion, author, and motivational speaker

Tip 85

A difficult time can be more readily endured if we retain the conviction that our existence holds a purpose — a cause to pursue, a person to love, a goal to achieve.

— John Maxwell, author, public speaker, and pastor

Think about your goals every day. Believe in them. Revisit the reasons why you came to this country. This will make it easy to face the challenges.

Tip 86

You can never quit. Winners never quit, and quitters never win.

— Ted Turner, media mogul and entrepreneur

Don't quit. Never ever give up! If you give up, you will never reach your goals.

Tip 87

The starting point of all achievement is desire. Keep this constantly in mind. Weak desires bring weak results, just as a small fire makes a small amount of heat.

— Napoleon Hill, author, journalist, salesman, and lecturer

You should aim for greater goals and constantly pursue them. The greater the goal, the greater the rewards.

Tip 88

Few people take objectives really seriously. They put average effort into too many things, rather than superior thought and effort into a few important things. People who achieve the most are selective as well as determined.

— Richard Koch, author, public speaker, investor, management consultant, and entrepreneur

Rather than tackle multiple things at the same time, begin by focusing your efforts on a single goal.

Tip 89

It's not what we do once in a while that shapes our lives. It's what we do consistently.

— Tony Robbins, performance coach, author, motivational speaker, and actor

You need to make a consistent effort to achieve success.

Tip 90

The only way to do great work is to love what you do. If you haven't found it yet, keep looking. Don't settle.

— Steve Jobs, entrepreneur, marketer, and inventor

If you haven't found your dream job, keep trying till you get it. Don't be satisfied with a survival job or staying at the same position in your current job.

Tip 91

You can make more friends in two months by becoming interested in other people than you can in two years by trying to get other people interested in you.

— Dale Carnegie, author and lecturer

Understand the difference between self-confidence and bragging. Listen attentively to others and show genuine interest in them.

Tip 92

Don't spend time beating on a wall, hoping to transform it into a door.

— Coco Chanel, fashion designer and entrepreneur

Sometimes it is better to design a Plan B. Continuing to focus on just one career option may mean unnecessary hardships.

Tip 93

The key is taking responsibility and initiative, deciding what your life is about and prioritizing your life around the most important things.

— Stephen Covey, educator, author, businessman, and public speaker

Choose your goals and prioritize your time and resources accordingly.

Tip 94

The quality of a person's life is in direct proportion to [his or her] commitment to excellence, regardless of [his or her] chosen field of endeavor.

— Vince Lombardi, football player, coach, and executive

Whatever field you pursue, your commitment to excellence determines the quality of life you will lead.

Tip 95

Be strong now because things will get better. It might be stormy now but it can't rain forever.

— Author unknown

Just like the sun emerges after the rain, hardship also passes. The fact is all immigrants can succeed. The challenge is how big the success is, and how long will it take! That is in your hands!

Tip 96

Nothing is predestined. The obstacles of your past can become the gateways that lead to new beginnings.

— Ralph Blum, author

Your fate is not predetermined. You have the power to create it. Transform obstacles into opportunities that lead to new pathways.

Tip 97

Nothing in this world can take the place of persistence.

Talent will not: Nothing is more common than unsuccessful men with talent. Genius will not; unrewarded genius is almost a proverb.

Education will not: The world is full of educated derelicts.

Persistence and determination alone are omnipotent.

— Calvin Coolidge, former president of the United States

So many of us give up far too soon. So many success stories are about persistence.

Tip 98

Intolerance of your present creates your future.

— Mike Murdock, evangelist, pastor, and author

Don't accept second best and get comfortable with it. Complacency is the enemy of progress.

Tip 99

Identify your problems but give your power and energy to solutions.

— Tony Robbins, performance coach, author, motivational speaker, and actor

Understand the problems and focus your energy and resources to solve them.

Tip 100

If you don't get noticed, you don't have anything. You just have to be noticed, but the art is in getting noticed naturally, without screaming or without tricks.

— Leo Burnett, advertising executive

Do an excellent job, take initiatives, and set an exemplary performance to make yourself visible.

Tip 101

Too many of us are not living our dreams because we are living our fears.

— Les Brown, motivational speaker, former politician, author, and radio DJ

The more you dwell on your fears, the more you weaken your efforts to accomplish your goals.

Tip 102

No one is going to hand me success. I must go out and get it myself. That's why I'm here. To dominate. To conquer. Both the world, and myself.

— Author unknown

Success is not achieved without effort. You came here to find a better life. Now take that goal from your mind and make it a reality.

Tip 103

Remember that not getting what you want is sometimes a wonderful stroke of luck.

— Dalai Lama, spiritual leader

If Plan A doesn't work, move onto Plan B which might become instrumental to your success.

Tip 104

Wherever you go, no matter what the weather, always bring your own sunshine.

— Anthony J. D'Angelo, author

Every one of us has unique traits in our personality and we should always carry these good qualities with us.

Tip 105

Your attitudes and the choices you make today will be your life tomorrow, build it wisely.

— Author unknown

We should not act and behave with only immediate gains in mind as today's decisions will shape our future.

Tip 106

I take compliments and I take constructive criticism. Not everyone loves you. It's the way you react as a footballer. I use it all to make me play better.

— Timothy F. Cahill, football player

Use constructive criticism to continuously improvement yourself.

Tip 107

Embrace your new country. Fall in love with it. Explore its history, its people, and its beauty for then, you will truly find home!

— Nick (Naeem) Noorani, immigrant champion, author, and motivational speaker

Tip 108

As you climb the ladder of success, check occasionally to make sure it is leaning against the right wall.

— Author unknown

While working your way towards your goals, it is important that you do periodic checks on whether your hard work is influencing results in the right direction. While looking for a job, understand what the recruiters expect and then customize your résumé. Assessing your education qualifications against the set standards and matching your previous job roles to equivalent job titles in the host country are some of the things that you can do to create an impact.

Understand Your Strengths and Weaknesses

A couple of years ago, there was a survey conducted at a venue where both new Canadians and employers had gathered. In the survey, immigrants were asked "Do you think your lack of English language skills is a barrier to getting a job?" An overwhelming 87 percent said "no"! Employers were then asked whether immigrant language skills kept them from gainful employment and the answer was 95 percent "yes"!

Speaking to almost 2,000 immigrants a year I can safely say I agree with the fact that a substantial number of immigrants are not aware of their shortcomings, particularly in relation to their language ability and their credentials in the Canadian context. That becomes a problem because, if you don't know what you don't know, how can you correct it?

Not exclusive to migrants, fully understanding one's strengths and weaknesses and being truly self-aware is not always easy. As human beings, we often find it difficult to face up to reality, accept when we're wrong, admit to making mistakes, and acknowledge we may not be very good at something.

When people make mistakes, they often get defensive and become unwilling to change, rather than being open to new ways and ideas.

To thrive in a new country, it's critical to put down your defences and to objectively reassess your skills in a new light — a Canadian light. Sure, you may have had the best English skills among your friends and family in your country of origin, but are you at the level of a Canadian-born person? Likely not. You've made the huge change of leaving your home to build a new life, so it's not the time to be resistant to change after you arrive.

How should you go about assessing your strengths and weaknesses? Why not start with a simple list? Get a piece of paper and on one side, write two columns, with the headline "Current Strengths" at the top of one column, and the headline "Improvements needed for the Canadian Context." On the flip side, do the same for "Current Weaknesses."

Now be honest. Unless you are absolutely fluent in English, having learned it at an early age, I suggest the majority of immigrants put English skills as "Weaknesses" and list ways you can improve or adjust your skills in Canada. Focus also on all the typical "soft skills" that employers look for in Canada — positivity, communication skills, leadership, and initiative. Most newcomers don't have the type of soft skills Canadian employers are looking for.

Progress can only truly happen when you understand your starting point. Also, seek the help of settlement agency experts who can help you assess your strengths and weaknesses objectively.

Tip 109

The only place success comes before work is in the dictionary.

— Vince Lombardi, football player,
coach, and executive

Success is the sweet fruit of hard work, self-discipline, and perseverance. You may have to upgrade your knowledge and language skills. You may have to start at the bottom in your career, but look at the successful immigrants around you. They all got where they are with hard work and perseverance.

Tip 110

I don't believe you have to be better than everybody else. I believe you have to be better than you ever thought you could be.

— Ken Venturi, professional golfer and broadcaster

To succeed, you have to compete not as much with the others as with your own self. Don't view yourself at any sort of disadvantage to the natives. You possess skills, knowledge, and competencies that are equal or higher. Continuously reinventing yourself and your situations is the only way to leverage the opportunities coming your way. Find out ways to improve what you are doing today to make it better tomorrow.

Tip 111

I identify with Superman. I am adopted, I am an only child, and I love the idea that he comes from another world, that he's the ultimate immigrant. He has all these extraordinary powers, and he has righteousness about him.

— Bryan Singer, film director, writer, and producer

Consider yourself to be an alien in this new unknown land and find strength in your abilities and skills. Many immigrants tend to be better educated than native-born populations.

Tip 112

Each problem has hidden in it an opportunity so powerful that it literally dwarfs the problem. The greatest success stories were created by people who recognized a problem and turned it into an opportunity.

— Joseph Sugarman, author and public speaker

Scrutinize your problem from all sides and see if there is a way you can take advantage of it. In my life, my challenges with immigrating made me study it in depth and actually start effecting change in the lives of other immigrants.

Tip 113

Inaction creates nothing. Action creates success.

— Stephen Richards, author

If you don't act now, the challenges will continue. Be active and take steps to resolve each challenge one by one just the way you climb up the ladder one step at a time.

Tip 114

If we listened to our intellect, we'd never have a love affair. We'd never have a friendship. We'd never go into business because we'd be too cynical ... Well, that's nonsense. You've got to jump off cliffs all the time and build your wings on the way down.

— Ray Bradbury, author

Swimming can be learned only when we are in water. Similarly, you will acquire many new skills and competencies on the way. Don't be too self-critical; at times, going with your gut feeling creates greater rewards.

Tip 115

Wisdom is knowing what to do next, skills is knowing how to do it, and virtue is doing it.

— David Starr Jordan, ichthyologist, educator, eugenicist, and peace activist

Somewhere deep inside we know what needs to be done. All that holds us back is fear. Fear of the unknown? Or losing the little money you have? Conquer fear and success will hold you in its strong embrace.

Tip 116

Sit down before fact as a little child, be prepared to give up every preconceived notion, follow humble wherever and to whatever abysses nature leads, or you shall learn nothing.

— Thomas Henry Huxley, biologist

Accept the reality that technical skills can only take you as far as an interview. To get a job you need soft skills. Once you realize this fact, your mind will open to new learning and experiences.

Tip 117

Learning is a treasure that will follow its owner everywhere.

— Chinese Proverb

Soft skills, including communication, interpersonal, and negotiation learned once can be leveraged in all types of jobs as well as personal and professional situations.

Tip 118

Language is not a genetic gift, it is a social gift. Learning a new language is becoming a member of the club — the community of speakers of that language.

— Frank Smith, psycholinguist

Language skills are an important way to integrate into the workplace as well as the community. Enhance your skills and you'll reap the benefits of greater opportunities.

Tip 119

Don't use words too big for the subject. Don't say infinitely when you mean very; otherwise you'll have no word left when you want to talk about something really infinite.

— C.S. Lewis, author, academic, literary critic, and lay theologian

You should constantly work on improving your communication skills — both personal and professional. This will help you to impress your audience as well as effectively convey your ideas.

Tip 120

Do not go where the path may lead, go instead where there is no path and leave a trail.

— Ralph Waldo Emerson, author and lecturer

Many immigrants take big risks and are leaders. Look inside you. Is that who you are?

Tip 121

True happiness involves the full use of one's power and talents.

— John W. Gardner, former Secretary of Health, Education, and Welfare for the United States

While striving for your ambitions, utilize all your capabilities and strengths.

Tip 122

Great minds have purposes, others have wishes. Little minds are tamed and subdued by misfortune; but great minds rise above them.

— Washington Irving, author, editor, and diplomat

Focus your thoughts on your long-term goal. Don't be bogged down by a failure. Take criticism constructively. Work on your weak points, and strive to continually improve yourself.

Tip 123

We all have dreams. But in order to make dreams come into reality, it takes an awful lot of determination, dedication, self-discipline, and effort.

— Jesse Owens, athlete and Olympic gold medalist

It takes discipline and determination to translate your dreams into reality.

Tip 124

Some people think that in order for immigrants to succeed, they need to start at the bottom. I do not agree with this, but believe you should have a Plan B for your life in Canada. Plan B means having flexibility in what you intend to do in your new country. Use your transferable skills to create a viable Plan B

— Nick (Naeem) Noorani, immigrant champion, author, and motivational speaker

Tip 125

Believe in possibilities. Believe in human potential. Believe in yourself and you'll have the power to change your fate.

— Kevin Ngo, author

You have all the power, abilities, and resources to design your future.

Tip 126

We are the sum total of the five people closest to us. If you play with the Michael Jordans, you are bound to improve your moves!

— Nick (Naeem) Noorani, immigrant champion, author, and motivational speaker

Tip 127

Every experience in your life is being orchestrated to teach you something you need to know to move forward.

— Brian Tracy, entrepreneur, public speaker, author, and personal and professional development trainer

Carefully analyze every experience through meeting a stranger, a new work assignment, a coffee cooler discussion, or business lunch. In each experience there is a hidden lesson that can teach you what you need to continue growing.

Tip 128

The longer you're not taking action, the more money you're losing.

— Carrie Wilkerson, author, public speaker, podcaster, and professional radio guest

The faster you reach your goals, the more money you will make. The time wasted in indecision could have made you money.

Tip 129

I know you're smart. But everyone here is smart. Smart isn't enough. The kind of people I want on my research team are those who will help everyone feel happy to be here.

— Randy Pausch, professor

Employers don't want talent with just technical competence. They want people who can fit into their company's culture and build collaborative teams.

Tip 130

A winner is someone who recognizes his talents, works his tail off to develop them into skills, and uses these skills to accomplish his goals.

— Larry Bird, former professional basketball player and current team president of the Indiana Pacers

Set your target, work hard to enhance your soft skills, and then use these soft skills to achieve these targets.

Tip 131

Creativity, as has been said, consists largely of rearranging what we know in order to find out what we do not know. Hence, to think creatively, we must be able to look afresh at what we normally take for granted.

— George Kneller, critical theorist and author

Develop new perspectives to look at things. Use your knowledge, experience, and connections to find hidden opportunities.

Tip 132

The unexamined life is not worth living.

— Socrates, philosopher

Take time to assess your achievements and failures, strengths and weaknesses, and opportunities and threats.

Tip 133

There are four ways, and only four ways, in which we have contact with the world. We are evaluated and classified by these four contacts: What we do, how we look, what we say, and how we say it.

— Dale Carnegie, author and lecturer

Employers evaluate us based on four criteria: technical competence, personality, communication skills (i.e., verbal, body language, and presentation), and empathy.

Tip 134

Business today consists in persuading crowds.

— Gerald S. Lee, clergyman and author

Influencing and negotiating skills are highly valued at the workplace when dealing with clients, colleagues, and supervisors.

Tip 135

Good manners and soft words have brought many a difficult thing to pass.

— Sir John Vanbrugh, architect and dramatist

Rudeness accomplishes nothing and only alienates others. Be calm and thoughtful in the way you treat others.

5

Seek Help and Advice

Canada has an extensive network of resources and social programs, including hundreds of immigrant settlement agencies across the country that strive to help newcomers integrate and succeed in Canada. Such agencies offer everything from English as a Second Language (ESL) training, to family counselling, to résumé help. Often, these services are underutilized, as newcomers are shy to make use of such resources.

Seeking advice and help from others is the fastest, most efficient way to learn and adapt. The staff and counsellors at these agencies are experts in their fields, who know the ins and outs of immigrating and can help you with your questions. These types of services are funded by the government and are mostly free to you. You can find an extensive list of such services targeted to newcomers on the Government of Canada website (www.canada.ca) under "Immigration."

On a less formal level, I always encourage immigrants to seek advice from other Canadians, especially those who also walked down the immigration path and have reached success. In other words, seek some mentors. Whether you meet over a cup of coffee or sign up to get a mentor through a formal mentorship program offered via an immigrant settlement agency, find a person you can talk to about where you want to be and ask him or her questions on how he or she got there. The trick here is to find a mentor who has achieved something you hope to emulate.

After I arrived in Canada, I sought the mentorship of at least six different people who each possessed some knowledge or achievement I was hoping to reach myself. To this day, I still seek their input as I continue into the next phases of my personal journey as an immigrant, public speaker, and social entrepreneur. Plus, now I pay it forward by being a mentor to other more recent newcomers and sharing the wisdom I have learned from others.

I have come full circle, starting as a newcomer who was unsure and full of questions, to a success story who can guide the way for others. It is why I give my speeches and write my books; I want to be a source for you when you are seeking help.

Tip 136

I do not want my house to be walled in on all sides and my windows to be stuffed. I want the cultures of all the lands to be blown about my house as freely as possible. But I refuse to be blown off my feet by any.

— Mahatma Gandhi, leader of Indian Independence Movement, philosopher, and peaceful activist

Go out and network with people outside your own cultural or professional group. Appreciate the cultural diversity. Observe, incorporate, and integrate the new learning to improve your cultural fit. Start with community service programs, seminars, workshops, and discussion. You will realize this goes a long way in developing soft skills that are essential for successful employment. However, don't forget your heritage. Cultural fluency is not about losing your own heritage but adding to it to become more holistic.

Tip 137

Start where you are. Use what you have. Do what you can.

— Arthur Ashe, former professional tennis player

To shape your future, you should make a start today. Don't stay too long in a "survival" job. Make an action plan of how you would reach your target, what resources you have, and what additional support you require.

Tip 138

Education costs money. But then so does ignorance.

— Sir Claus Moser, Baron and statistician

Considering the financial and time constraints, enrolling in advanced language classes seems like a big challenge. However, lack of appropriate English language skills and cultural knowledge is also hindering your chances of good employment. Invest in courses that will improve your performance at work.

Tip 139

Don't go around saying the world owes you a living. The world owes you nothing. It was here first.

— Robert Jones Burdette

Your host country's government is not obligated to provide you a living. It has been and will always be there. Look for services by immigration agencies to support your endeavour, but ultimately it is you who will have to find the road to success.

Tip 140

Remember no one can make you feel inferior without your consent.

— Eleanor Roosevelt, politician and former first lady
of the United States

Moving to a new country will inevitably involve some acts of veiled racism or biases in workplaces. This may occur due to the vulnerability and uniqueness of newcomers. Don't be a silent victim to emotional hurt. Seek support from friends, family, and relatives; understand your rights and be upfront. Be wise, act maturely, and move forward.

Tip 141

Learn everything you can, anytime you can, from anyone you can; there will always come a time when you will be grateful you did.

— Sarah Caldwell, opera conductor, impresario, and stage director of opera

Learning is a continuous process. You should make use of all opportunities to learn skills and behaviour from various situations and people. It can accelerate your journey to success.

Tip 142

If you find yourself saying "But I can't speak English ... ," try adding the word "... yet."

— Jane Revell, author and trainer; and Susan Norman, author

Without perfecting your English skills, you cannot achieve your goals. Don't ignore this aspect any further. Enroll in English language classes that meet your requirements. Speak, listen, and read English or French eight hours a day for 90 days and I guarantee your English or French will improve dramatically. Trust me, this works!

Tip 143

The limits of my language mean the limits of my world.

— Ludwig Wittgenstein, philosopher

If you feel that your limited knowledge of the language is hindering your growth prospects, invest in yourself by enrolling in classes to boost your grammar and vocabulary.

Tip 144

There is only one rule for being a good talker — learn to listen.

— Christopher Morley, author and journalist

Good communication also includes active listening. Show interest in what others say by smiling, nodding, and making eye contact.

Tip 145

The key is to keep company only with people who uplift you, whose presence calls forth your best.

— Epictetus, philosopher

My favorite saying is, "We are the sum total of the five people closest to us." Who are your five?

Tip 146

Researchers have settled on what they believe is the magic number for true expertise: ten thousand hours.

— Malcolm Gladwell, author and journalist

Read Malcolm Gladwell's *Outliers: The Story of Success*. He talks about investing 10,000 hours to become a subject matter expert. How are you investing in yourself?

Tip 147

If I have the belief that I can do it, I shall surely acquire the capacity to do it even if I may not have it at the beginning.

— Mahatma Gandhi, leader of Indian Independence Movement, philosopher, and peaceful activist

If you are passionate about success, learn the skills which you don't have.

Tip 148

If you come off as someone who knows everything — or you think you do — many people will back away. If you want to learn, be willing to consider ideas that may not match your expectations or opinions.

— Author unknown

Bragging puts off other people. Approach others with an open mind and listen to their ideas.

Tip 149

Be sure to set your sights on someone who could be a good role model, someone who has the skills and personality that match your chemistry.

— Martin Zwilling, entrepreneur.com

Seek someone from a similar field and experience who can be your mentor. Mentors can change your life in a new country.

Tip 150

As they say, advice is cheap, but mentorship is worth its weight in gold.

— Amy Errett, entrepreneur

Rather than take everyone's advice, rely on a mentor who is successful and can speak from his or her own experiences to support you and boost your spirits.

Tip 151

It's not what you know but who you know that makes the difference.

— Author unknown

As immigrants, we leave all our established networks behind and have to learn the science of creating new networks. Networking helps you discover hidden job opportunities and information on career prospects. You may also find your mentor through networking.

Tip 152

Best results are often achieved well before you need a job, by consistently networking so that when you find yourself job-hunting you have a large network to work with.

— Erik Qualman, author, professor, and public speaker

An increasing number of employers are filling their job vacancies by referrals. It is always good to network with people who can act as sources for hidden job openings.

Tip 153

The richest people in the world look for and build networks, everyone else looks for work.

— Robert Kiyosaki, author, investor, entrepreneur, motivational speaker, and financial literacy activist

Human capital is the key to business success today. Create and nurture a strong network of important people.

Tip 154

For every one of us that succeeds, it's because there's somebody there to show you the way out.

— Oprah Winfrey, television host, actress, CEO, and author

Seek a mentor from your personal or professional networks to guide you through his or her own experience and learning.

Tip 155

If you want to go somewhere, it is best to find someone who has already been there.

— Robert Kiyosaki, author, investor, entrepreneur, motivational speaker, and financial literacy activist

A mentor is the best person to guide and lead your efforts in the right direction because he or she has seen and knows a lot.

Tip 156

The important thing is to concentrate upon what you can do — by yourself, upon your own initiative.

— Harry Browne, author, politician, and investment analyst

Take classes and courses to learn soft skills. Observe others and participate in workplace discussions, meetings, and events to enhance your interpersonal skills.

Tip 157

A smart man makes a mistake, learns from it, and never makes that mistake again. But a wise man finds a smart man and learns from him how to avoid the mistake altogether.

— Roy H. Williams, author and marketing consultant

Why do we like to read about successful people? So we can learn from them! Fill your life with positive and successful role models and you will become one too.

Tip 158

Formal education will make you a living; self-education will make you a fortune.

— Jim Rohn, entrepreneur, author, and motivational speaker

Your technical skills can take you only as far as a job interview or offer, but networking, volunteering, and getting a mentor will empower your success.

Tip 159

If you ain't making waves, you ain't kicking hard enough.

— Author unknown

If you are unable to make desired changes, then it is possible that your efforts are weak. Boost the power of your efforts by learning and developing skills that will help you.

Tip 160

Keep on the lookout for novel ideas that others have used successfully. Your idea has to be original only in its adaptation to the problem you're working on.

— Thomas Edison, inventor and entrepreneur

Learn from other people who were in a similar position in the past and emerged successful. Use this knowledge to resolve specific problems.

Tip 161

Change. Adapt. Bend so as not to be broken. Let opportunity guide your actions.

— Wayne Gerard Trotman, author, filmmaker, photographer, and music composer and producer

Adapt to meet the demands of the job market. Let employer expectations guide you in selecting what you need to learn to improve your prospects.

Tip 162

Education is not the piling on of learning, information, data, facts, skills, or abilities — that's training or instruction — but is rather making visible what is hidden as a seed.

— Thomas Moore, poet, singer,
songwriter, and entertainer

Make your knowledge and experience visible to others by seeking opportunities at and outside of work.

Tip 163

I think that if you keep your eyes and your ears open and you are receptive to learning, there are skills you can get from any job at all.

— Cat Deeley, television presenter,
actress, singer, and model

During your first year, be a sponge! Absorb information by observing your surroundings and being open to learning. There are several things you can learn from everyday experiences at the workplace and in regular life.

Tip 164

Perhaps one of the simplest strategies for avoiding conflict is knowing when to stop fighting back.

— Nick (Naeem) Noorani, immigrant champion,
author, and motivational speaker

Learn conflict-resolution strategies for business success and build long-term relationships. Remember, sometimes it is better to just walk away.

Tip 165

He who would learn to fly one day must first learn to stand and walk and run and climb and dance; one cannot fly into flying.

— Friedrich Nietzsche, philologist, philosopher, cultural critic, poet, and composer

Like a child learning to walk, you must learn new skills and improve your English or French in order to acquire your dream job in Canada.

Tip 166

I like to listen. I have learned a great deal from listening carefully. Most people never listen.

— Ernest Hemingway, author and journalist

Listening is an art. It is sometimes a challenge for many immigrants. Stop and listen. Give attention and a positive response when others talk.

Tip 167

Being ignorant is not so much a shame, as being unwilling to learn.

— Benjamin Franklin, one of the Founding Fathers of the United States, author, postmaster, scientist, inventor, activist, and diplomat

Don't find excuses not to invest in learning skills critical for success.

Tip 168

To be a winner in life and in business you must act like a winner, and what better way to do that than to emulate the habits of highly successful people.

— Peter Legge, chairman, CEO, and publisher

Read and emulate the greatest successes of our time.

Tip 169

The best preparation for good work tomorrow is to do good work today.

— Elbert Hubbard, author, publisher, artist, and philosopher

Learn and develop soft skills so that you not only get your dream job but can be the best at it.

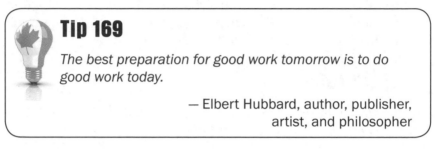

Tip 170

Asking questions is a big part of the learning process.

— Nick (Naeem) Noorani, immigrant champion, author, and motivational speaker

Don't be afraid to ask your employer questions. Clarify expectations and what is not clear to you.

Tip 171

First, have a definite, clear practical ideal; a goal, an objective. Second, have the necessary means to achieve your ends; wisdom, money, materials, and methods. Third, adjust all your means to that end.

— Aristotle, philosopher and scientist

Focus all your resources to achieve your ultimate goal. Invest money and time to learn new skills. Most of all, embrace an open mindset and make an effort to meet new people and build long-term relationships.

Tip 172

Want to achieve abundance? Surround yourself with career mentors and experts; this is a shortcut to success. Be a life-long student of both personal and professional growth and development — stay inspired and hungry to live and lead an extraordinary life instead of an ordinary one.

— Praveen Varshney, entrepreneur

Mentorship is important to continually learn. Varshney has been my mentor for 15 years!

Tip 173

In the end we only regret the chances we didn't take, the relationships we were afraid to have, and the decisions we waited too long to make. Don't waste a single moment.

— Author unknown

Take risks, don't hesitate to initiate a conversation with colleagues and friends from other communities, and don't wait for situations to become favourable on their own.

Tip 174

Good manners will open doors that the best education cannot.

— Clarence Thomas, Associate Justice of the Supreme Court of the United States

If you behave courteously to your peers and seniors, your attitude will strike a rapport with others and make you more comfortable in an unfamiliar environment.

Tip 175

You are your greatest asset. Put your time, effort, and money into training, grooming, and encouraging your greatest asset.

— Tom Hopkins, businessperson

Invest time, effort, and money to improve your language skills. Network and volunteer to learn soft skills and understand the principles of body language.

Tip 176

Give me six hours to chop down a tree and I will spend the first four sharpening the axe.

— Abraham Lincoln, former President
of the United States

Learn soft skills, which are the greatest determinant of your success.

6
Accept Rejection

No one, and I mean no one, likes to be rejected. However, in today's highly competitive economy, there is more than a high chance that you will face rejection at some point in your career.

The typical scenario of a recent newcomer goes something like this: You arrive, send hundreds of résumés to a variety of employers, hope to get a response and you don't, so you feel rejected. You start blaming the country and all the external factors that have resulted in your rejection. To some extent, you are correct. There are certain things you do not have control over that will lead to your being rejected — systemic discrimination in the workplace, risk-averse employers, and lack of contacts.

Even once you're in the workplace, you'll find rejection at every corner. You may get passed over for a promotion, a colleague may dislike you (it happens even to the nicest of us!), your immediate supervisor may criticize your work, or you may even get fired or laid off (that happened to me right after I bought my first home in Canada). Accept that you don't have control over these things, and accept that rejection may come along with them. That doesn't mean you have to like it, but you can do something about it.

As I said, while there are things you don't have control over, there are plenty of things you do have control over. One is how you handle the rejection. Are you being victimized by it? Are you lashing out and becoming belligerent? Or are you focusing on finding positive solutions that you can control? You can improve your English language competency, network to make contacts in your industry, and focus on continuing professional development to keep your skills sharp and yourself inspired.

We all face rejection many times in life, and immigrants don't corner the market on it alone. Whether it's your career or your personal life, the difference between long-term success and failure is not whether you face rejection, it's how you choose to deal with it when it does occur. I like to say that the difference between a successful person and an unsuccessful one is that the successful person kept picking himself or herself up and trying again. Eventually, you will reach your goals. The unsuccessful person gave up before he or she had the opportunity. You never know if your very next attempt could result in success!

Tip 177

I'm very inspired by him — it was my father who taught us that an immigrant must work twice as hard as anybody else, that he must never give up.

— Zinedine Zidane, soccer player

All immigrants have to work harder than natives because they not only have to earn money to support themselves but also to gain an equivalent social status.

Tip 178

Baby, we have no choice of what colour we're born or who our parents are or whether we're rich or poor. What we do have is some choice over what we make of our lives once we're here.

— Mildred D. Taylor, author

Spend time with people who value you for who you are. Don't make apologies for speaking with an accent. Those who are really smart will look beyond these barriers to see your intellect and the person you are.

Tip 179

Body language is a very powerful tool. We had body language before we had speech. The world's best business communicators have strong body language: a commanding presence that reflects confidence, competence, and charisma. Eighty percent of what you understand in a conversation is read through the body, not the words.

— Author unknown

Be watchful of how you carry yourself before others. Develop the ability to read signs and signals of non-verbal communication. This will help you empathize and effectively communicate with others.

Tip 180

First they ignore you, then they ridicule you, then they fight you, and then you win.

— Often attributed to Mahatma Gandhi, leader of Indian Independence Movement, philosopher and peaceful activist

People might not recognise your skills or they might treat you differently because of your accent or how you dress. However, you should continue on your path of learning and improvement. Your technical skills give you the competitive advantage; you just have to polish your soft skills. Once you do that, you will gain what you truly deserve.

Tip 181

I have not failed. I've just found 10,000 ways that won't work.

— Thomas Edison, inventor and entrepreneur

You should keep trying until you win. Don't take failure too seriously; learn from it and move forward.

Tip 182

The pessimist sees difficulty in every opportunity. The optimist sees the opportunity in every difficulty.

— Often attributed to Sir Winston Churchill

Build a positive attitude.

Tip 183

Nothing spendid has ever been achieved except by those who dared believe that something inside them was superior to circumstance.

— Bruce Barton, author,
advertising executive, and politician

Successful people have always achieved their dreams by rising above their circumstances. Remember, you are much stronger than the obstacles.

Tip 184

Smile even through your tears. Strong even through your fears.

— Author unknown

A positive attitude is the best way to overcome challenges and obstacles.

Tip 185

History has demonstrated that the most notable winners usually encountered heartbreaking obstacles before they triumphed. They won because they refused to become discouraged by their defeats.

— Bertie Charles Forbes, financial journalist and author

Don't let rejections and failures dampen your spirits. The ability to get up and face a challenge is the strength of winners.

Tip 186

A successful man is one who can lay a firm foundation with the bricks others have thrown at him.

— David Brinkley, newscaster

Take constructive criticism seriously. Improve workplace skills such as communication or presentation skills if they are obstacles preventing you from greater achievements.

Tip 187

One of the most common causes of failure is the habit of quitting when one is overtaken by temporary defeat.

— Napoleon Hill, author, journalist, salesman, and lecturer

Interview rejections and negative feedback at the workplace should not be cause to abandon your journey to success. You only need to understand the reasons, make improvements, and continue.

Tip 188

Being defeated is often a temporary condition. Giving up is what makes it permanent.

— Marilyn vos Savant, magazine columnist, author, lecturer, and playwright

Failure is just a temporary phase. You can overcome it by working smart and hard.

Tip 189

Don't be afraid to fail. Don't waste energy trying to cover up failure. Learn from your failures and go on to the next challenge. It's OK to fail. If you're not failing, you're not growing.

— H. Stanley Judd, author

Failures are lessons. Make improvements and continue with your action plan.

Tip 190

If you don't believe you'll be able to succeed and overcome the challenges of being an immigrant, you will never really try. Avoid complaining and commiserating with other immigrants about discrimination you think you face. It's not productive for your success.

— Nick (Naeem) Noorani, immigrant champion, author, and motivational speaker

Tip 191

Every great personal story you have to tell involves overcoming adversity. If you shy away from adversity, you take away your ability to tell new stories.

— Farrel Droke, musician

Read about any success story and you will find winners are always made after they've overcome hardships. It is not easy yet not impossible. Don't run away from challenges.

Tip 192

Great spirits have always encountered violent opposition from mediocre minds.

— Albert Einstein, physicist and philosopher of science

This saying holds a special meaning for me as it was on my father's desk. Don't be afraid to turn away from closed minds or defeatist attitudes, as they may be envious of the potential they see in you.

Tip 193

The real man smiles in trouble, gathers strength from distress, and grows brave by reflection.

— Thomas Paine, political activist, philosopher, political theorist, and revolutionary

Challenges and barriers have many lessons to be learned if you look carefully. Reflect on them and analyze the underlying reasons. Invest to improve your skills and abilities to leverage the next set of opportunities. Just never give up!

Tip 194

Most great people have attained their greatest success just one step beyond their greatest failure.

— Napoleon Hill, author, journalist, salesman, and lecturer

Don't quit. You might be just a step away from your success. There is a story about a gold miner who quit inches away from his goal; he sold his mine only to have the newcomers strike it rich the same day.

Tip 195

Good humor is the health of the soul, sadness is its poison.

— Lord Chesterfield, 4th Earl of Chesterfield, British Statesman, and Man of Letters

Stay positive even in tough times. This keeps you motivated. Pessimistic and gloomy attitudes kill your opportunities to success.

Tip 196

Challenges are what make life interesting; overcoming them is what makes life meaningful.

— Joshua J. Marine, author

You will stagnate without any challenges. The obstacles you learn to overcome give meaning to your life.

Tip 197

Success consists of going from failure to failure without loss of enthusiasm.

— Sir Winston Churchill, former Prime Minister of the United Kingdom

Use failure as a motivation to succeed.

Tip 198

He who has learned to disagree without being disagreeable has discovered the most valuable secret of a diplomat.

— Robert Estabrook, journalist

Voice your opinion at work in a polite and respectful manner. Stick to the facts and avoid personal remarks.

Tip 199

The most difficult thing in any negotiation, almost, is making sure that you strip it of the emotion and deal with the facts.

— Howard Baker, Jr., politician and diplomat

Fact-based discussions help you make your point with more conviction and confidence. Emotional discussions tend to divert from the subject.

Tip 200

During a negotiation, it would be wise not to take any-thing personally. If you leave personalities out of it, you will be able to see opportunities more objectively.

— Brian Koslow, author

Don't let your ego influence your actions and arguments in a discussion. Focus on the subject of the negotiation rather than taking things personally, as an opportunity to prove yourself.

Tip 201

Just because you're miserable doesn't mean you can't enjoy your life.

— Annette Goodheart, author

Don't allow negativity to destroy your initiative and enthusiasm.

Tip 202

To be a star, you must shine your own light, follow your own path, and don't worry about the darkness, for that is when the stars shine brightest.

— Author unknown

Challenges enrich your talents and abilities and shape you into a better person. Keep pursuing your dreams.

7

Embrace Change

In all the chapters up to now, you'll notice one consistent theme — change. You have made a huge leap of faith by immigrating to Canada. You've left your country of birth, your family, your friends, your established career, and everything that is familiar and comfortable. This is what I call your "comfort zone." Interestingly, after making such a huge change by immigrating to a new country, newcomers often try to recreate that comfort zone in Canada. They speak their home languages, they settle in ethnic-focused communities, and they mix among people that came from the same countries of birth as they did.

Why did you bother coming to a new country? Ask yourself what propelled you to leave everything behind for this new adventure called Canadian immigration. Were you looking for something different, a change?

Why stop now? Remember your dreams about coming to Canada? Well, they have come true. Unfortunately, it's all too common that after newcomers arrive, they are initially disappointed. In my experience working with newcomers, too many immigrants keep dwelling on their previous lives and glorifying them. I call this driving with your eye firmly on the rear-view mirror! What happens when you don't keep your eyes on the road ahead? You will crash!

Does that sound familiar? Well, stop it! Unless you plan on returning to your homeland, there is no point in doing this, is there? Focus on the positive, and embrace your new country and all the changes your journey has brought with it.

Despite some real challenges of adapting to a new country, you have the chance for a fresh start. Isn't that what you wanted? Embrace the change!

Tip 203

Sometimes we stare so long at a door that is closing that we see too late the one that is open.

— Alexander Graham Bell, scientist, inventor, engineer, and innovator

Accept all the new things around you, and make changes in your way of life to create a new identity for yourself.

Tip 204

Change is the essence of life. Be willing to surrender what you are for what you could become.

— Author Unknown

Until you let go of your old habits, there will be no room for newer experiences. You came to this country with a dream of becoming a success. I often tell immigrants that those who succeed are those who understand that they are now in a new country. What worked in your old country may not work here. Discover what works in your new country.

Tip 205

When I let go of what I am, I become what I might be.

— Lao-Tzu, philosopher and poet

To adapt and accept the new environment, immigrants have to change the way they think, and their behaviour, habits, and social norms. This requires both accurate knowledge and willingness to adopt the new rules.

Tip 206

Comfort zones are like a snug, cozy bed on a winter morning; easy to get into, but hard to get out of!

— Nick (Naeem) Noorani, immigrant champion, author, and motivational speaker

The very act of immigration is moving out of your comfort zone. Immigrants leave all that they know to go to a land that they know very little about. You may have found a job that may not match your education and experience but gives you a good stable source of income. This might give you gratification for a while but perhaps is not what you aspired for. Don't stop your struggle because you did not come here for comfort, but success.

Tip 207

When I was five years old, my mother always told me that happiness was the key to life. When I went to school, they asked me what I wanted to be when I grew up. I wrote down "happy." They told me I didn't understand the assignment, and I told them they didn't understand life.

— John Lennon, musician, singer, songwriter, and artist

Life is all about being happy anytime, anywhere, and with anyone. Coming to this new country is a decision you have made for better happier life for yourself and your family. Why let circumstances prove your decision wrong? Smile at the challenge, whatever it is, and say, "I am happy"!

Tip 208

You can never cross the ocean until you have the courage to lose sight of the shore.

— Christopher Columbus, maritime explorer

Staying in familiar surroundings can ensure your survival but to be successful you will have to move out of your comfort zone.

Tip 209

If you don't like something, change it. If you can't change it, change your attitude.

— Maya Angelou, author, dancer, actress, and singer

I meet many BMW immigrants. No, not the vehicle! BMW stands for "Bitch, Moan, and Whine": Immigrants who constantly complain about everything in their new country. This attitude will hold you back from success and you must change this to succeed.

Tip 210

Let the refining and improving of your own life keep you so busy that you have little time to criticize others.

— H. Jackson Brown, Jr., author

Criticizing government policies, employers' responses, and locals' attitudes will not help you. Invest time and effort in improving your language skills and understanding cultural differences.

Tip 211

You cannot tailor-make the situations in life but you can tailor-make the attitudes to fit those situations.

— Zig Ziglar, author, salesman, and motivational speaker

We cannot design life's challenges but we can certainly wear an attitude that takes the world in our stride.

Tip 212

The greatest discovery of all time is that a person can change his future by merely changing his attitude.

— Oprah Winfrey, television host, actress, CEO, and author

The way we react to life's events and situations either empowers us or makes us fearful. Despite encountering difficulties, if we focus our energy on finding solutions to problems, we unlock our potential to change our future.

Tip 213

Get going. Move forward. Aim High. Plan a takeoff. Don't just sit on the runway and hope someone will come along and push the airplane. It simply won't happen. Change your attitude and gain some altitude. Believe me, you'll love it up here.

— Donald Trump, entrepreneur, television personality, and author

Don't wait for anything or anyone to come and change your situation. Policies, procedures, and people's perceptions or attitudes won't change. Government, friends, or relatives can't hand you a job on a silver platter. It's only you who has to act to make it happen.

Tip 214

You cannot expect to achieve new goals or move beyond your present circumstances unless you change.

— Les Brown, motivational speaker, former politician, author, and radio DJ

Change means moving out of a comfort zone. Immigrants move out of their comfort zones by the very act of immigrating, but after immigrating, they no longer want to change or make an effort to integrate. Why? Ask yourself what you need to improve in yourself in order to succeed!

Tip 215

Progress is impossible without change, and those who cannot change their minds cannot change anything.

— George Bernard Shaw, playwright, critic, and political activist

A change in mindset is crucial to progress. Develop a positive attitude that affirms you can overcome all difficulties; this is the only way to break through mental barriers and move forward toward success.

Tip 216

Change the changeable, accept the unchangeable, and remove yourself from the unacceptable.

— Denis Waitley, author, consultant, and motivational speaker

Improve your language skills, accept a survival job to manage finances for the time being, and as soon as possible, move on from that survival job because that is not what you have come here for.

Tip 217

The only way to make sense out of change is to plunge into it, move with it, and join the dance.

— Alan W. Watts, philosopher, author, and public speaker

Don't be a mere spectator as your new life unfolds. Understand what is expected of you, learn new skills, make modifications, and enjoy your life in the new country.

Tip 218

I don't make friends based on where they come from or their ethnicity. I make friends based on where they are going.

— Nick (Naeem) Noorani, immigrant champion, author, and motivational speaker

Ethnic or cultural backgrounds should not be the criteria when it comes to choosing friends, otherwise you will restrict your interaction and learning to your ethnic enclave. The most successful immigrants have friends outside of their ethnic communities. Look for friends who share your dreams, passions, and desires. This will accelerate the journey to your destination.

Tip 219

As you discover what strength you can draw from your community in this world from which It stands apart, look outward as well as inward. Build bridges instead of walls.

— Sonia Sotomayor, Associate Justice of the Supreme Court of the United States

However comfortable it may feel, avoid remaining in ethnic ghettos. Make multicultural friends from various communities. This will prove resourceful, help you understand different cultures, and improve your communication and customer service skills.

Tip 220

If what you're doing isn't working, try something else!

— Unknown

Plan B happens when Plan A doesn't work. Unfortunately, that happens more often than you would think! For many immigrants, Plan B offers flexibility and a new possibility to achieve personal and professional success. Focus on your transferable skills when you create your Plan B.

Tip 221

The more I travelled, the more I realized that fear makes strangers of people who should be friends.

— Shirley MacLaine, actress, singer, dancer, author, and activist

Don't be afraid or shy away from interaction with colleagues from other ethnicities. Avoid ethnic ghettos and make friends with non-immigrants. Also avoid the invisible immigrant syndrome at workplaces.

Tip 222

It wasn't raining when Noah built the ark.

— Howard Ruff, financial adviser and author

When innovators are called "ahead of their time," it means they anticipate trends and needs. Start to learn and develop skills now so you can adapt to change.

Tip 223

A mind is like a parachute. It doesn't work if it isn't open.

— Frank Zappa, musician, singer, songwriter, composer, recording engineer, record producer, and film director

Open your mind to accept new realities.

Tip 224

The happiness of your life depends upon the quality of your thoughts.

— Marcus Aurelius, Roman Emperor

What you think has a huge impact on your attitude. Keep your thoughts positive to put your energy to best use.

Tip 225

When you have friends of all nationalities, you will learn a lot more. Research shows immigrants who live in ethnic silos and use their native language have a lower than average income!

— Nick (Naeem) Noorani, immigrant champion, author, and motivational speaker

Tip 226

People are always blaming their circumstances for what they are. I don't believe in circumstances. The people who get on in this world are the people who get up and look for the circumstances they want, and if they can't find them, they make them.

— George Bernard Shaw, playwright, critic, and political activist

Success comes to those who work hard to change their circumstances and not to those who complain about being a victim.

Tip 227

Some men have thousands of reasons why they cannot do what they want to, when all they need is one reason why they can.

— Mary Frances Berry, professor and former Chairwoman of the United States Commission on Civil Rights

I get upset when I see immigrants who know they need to enhance their language skills but think they can just get by without doing so. Language fluency is critical for success, so make it a priority.

Tip 228

Some immigrants keep dwelling on their lives before immigrating and glorifying it to make them feel important. While I understand this helps especially when highly skilled immigrants are doing dead-end jobs far below their skill sets, this action is counterproductive and will only hamper the immigrants' chances of success. I call it driving with your eye firmly on the rear-view mirror! You will crash! Remember the windshield is always larger and more relevant.

— Nick (Naeem) Noorani, immigrant champion, author, and motivational speaker

Tip 229

Inaction breeds doubt and fear. Action breeds confidence and courage. If you want to conquer fear, do not sit home and think about it. Go out and get busy.

— Dale Carnegie, author and lecturer

Overcome your fears and apprehensions by accepting the change with an open mind and making sincere efforts to adapt to the new environment. This will give you confidence and courage.

Tip 230

Immigrants must have flexibility! Remember, the average North American worker changes careers at least three to five times in his or her life. This means that you will likely never stop training and searching for a job. Given that the median year a person stays in one job is 4.1 years, an average person will have to have 7 to 10 jobs in their life.

— Nick (Naeem) Noorani, immigrant champion, author, and motivational speaker

Tip 231

The wise adapt themselves to circumstances, as water moulds itself to the pitcher.

— Chinese Proverbs

The way water takes the shape of any container it is poured into is the way you should adapt to the new situations.

Tip 232

The measure of intelligence is the ability to change.

— Albert Einstein, physicist and philosopher of science

Be flexible and adapt to the new environment, culture, and circumstances.

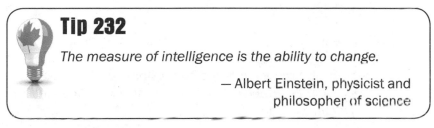

Tip 233

Enjoying success requires the ability to adapt. Only be being open to change will you have a true opportunity to get the most from your talent.

— Nolan Ryan, former professional baseball player and current executive adviser to the owner of the Houston Astros

Be flexible to adapt to new things. This is the only way to realize your full potential and leverage the opportunities.

Tip 234

If you'll not settle for anything less than your best, you will be amazed at what you can accomplish in your lives.

— Vince Lombardi, football player, coach, and executive

If you accept change and adapt to meet the challenges, you will get what you rightfully deserve.

Tip 235

Mental toughness is essential to success.

— Vince Lombardi, football player, coach, and executive

Resist negative thinking. The strength to endure any hardship is important to achieve your goals.

Tip 236

Too many people go through life complaining about their problems. I've always believed that if you took one tenth the energy you put into complaining and applied it to solving the problem, you'd be surprised by how well things can work out.

— Randy Pausch, professor

Rather than complaining, use your energy to solve problems and improve your situation faster.

Tip 237

Any fool can criticize, condemn, and complain but it takes character and self-control to be understanding and forgiving.

— Dale Carnegie, author and lecturer

This simple saying is so hard to follow, but make it something you practise doing and see how wonderful life can be.

Tip 238

Be the change you wish to see in the world.

— Mahatma Gandhi, leader of Indian Independence Movement, philosopher and peaceful activist

So many of us are armchair critics! Get off that sofa and do something about the changes you want. If you cannot be a part of the solution, you are a part of the problem.

Tip 239

There is this mythology that says that when people are born, their brains are essentially fixed very early on and they're not able to change their connections. I was aware that was a myth and that people could learn new skills.

— Daniel Tammet, author and translator

Ignore people and sayings that are designed to limit your potential in life. You can always learn new skills.

Tip 240

It is not the strongest or the most intelligent who will survive but those who can best manage change.

— Charles Darwin, naturalist and geologist

Put aside your conventional ways of thinking and adopt a more open mind to achieve your goals.

Tip 241

No one can be right 100 percent of the time. Yes, not even you!

— Nick (Naeem) Noorani, immigrant champion, author, and motivational speaker

Don't be rigid with your views; be flexible to accept others' ideas and learn from them.

Tip 242

Change will not come if we wait for some other person or some other time. We are the ones we have been waiting for. We are the change that we seek.

— President Barack Obama, President of the United States and Civil Rights Attorney

No one else but *you* can bring the change you seek. Adapt the culture of your new country and continue to learn new things.

Tip 243

You can't fall if you don't climb. But there's no joy in living your whole life on the ground.

— Author unknown

Break out of your comfort zone if you expect to attain your goal and push yourself to the maximum.

Tip 244

Stay committed to your decisions, but stay flexible in your approach.

— Tony Robbins

Stay firm on the decisions you have made, but while making your decisions, keep an open and flexible mind. This enables you to stick to your goals even if the situation has changed.

Tip 245

The survival of the fittest is the ageless law of nature, but the fittest are rarely the strong. The fittest are those endowed with the qualifications for adaptation, the ability to accept the inevitable and conform to the unavoidable, to harmonize with existing or changing conditions.

— Charles Darwin, naturalist and geologist

Being fit to win isn't just about physical strength. Quick adaptability to changing circumstances and the ability to foresee and be prepared for adverse situations are critical to overcoming challenges.

Tip 246

Many immigrants resist change and this becomes something that holds them back from reaching their maximum potential. You embraced change by immigrating. Continue that process and embrace the challenges that come with it.

— Nick (Naeem) Noorani, immigrant champion,
author, and motivational speaker

Tip 247

When you are frustrated and do not know a way out, only flexibility and moderation towards difficulties will save you.

— al-Husayn ibn, third Shia Imam

When you are stuck in a tough situation, don't panic. Think about the issue with an open mind and be willing to try non-conventional ways.

Tip 248

The keys to patience are acceptance and faith. Accept things as they are, and look realistically at the world around you. Have faith in yourself and in the direction you have chosen.

— Ralph Marston, author

Accept the reality that you need to change and adapt to the culture and mindset of your new country. Have faith in your dreams and your capabilities. Follow them patiently until you achieve your goals.

Tip 249

It is not the strongest or the most intelligent who will survive but those who can best manage change.

— Charles Darwin, naturalist and geologist

Adaptability and flexibility are key to achieving a successful career. This is much more important than technical skills.

Tip 250

All the art of living lies in a fine mingling of letting go and holding on.

— Henry Ellis, explorer and author

The art of adapting to new situations lies in releasing your old beliefs and embracing new ones.

8

Show Initiative

I've talked about embracing change and moving out of your comfort zone and seeking help. All of these are part and parcel of the concept of taking initiative. As an immigrant, you need to do things differently in your new country because what worked in your home country probably will not work here.

Showing initiative is a highly valued soft skill in Canada. People who take initiative are considered "go-getters" and will likely be the ones who get the job, get promoted, and achieve success faster. It's not about being aggressive, it's about being assertive, standing up and asking for what you want, and often finding your own solutions.

As a newcomer it's up to you to take the initiative to get the information you need to settle in, get the help you require, make connections, and help you get your credentialing done so you can get a job.

Once you find a job, showing initiative will be critical for how you're perceived by your employers. People who wait around to be told what to do and do not provide any input are not valued highly. Do not be a wallflower at meetings! Listen carefully, give your point of view, offer suggestions, and back them up with clear effort.

There is risk involved, as some people might not like your ideas, but don't let the risk of criticism stop you. Insulate yourself against negative thoughts. Connect with positive people.

Remember that in Canada you can be anyone you want. You can create the canvas of your life in the size that you want. You can have a postage stamp life or a life as big and as wide as this beautiful country.

Tip 251

The best time to look for a job is when you have a job!

— Nick (Naeem) Noorani, immigrant champion, author, and motivational speaker

Many of us might have to settle for a lower rung job to get that all important experience. If you are one of those employees, don't take your eyes off the ultimate goal. This first job is only a small stepping stone to get you started. Keep looking for work until you find the job that matches your level of qualifications, experience, and expectations. Don't get stuck in a survival job. Research has proven that if an immigrant stays in a survival job more than six months, he or she may stay there forever.

Tip 252

Volunteers are not paid — not because they are worthless, but because they are priceless.

— Sherry Andersen, author

Start volunteering your time. Most successful immigrants believe that it is the most rewarding experience when they are new to a country. Amidst all the homesickness, loneliness, and culture shock, volunteering gives the satisfaction of helping others, making friends, learning the new culture, and enhancing skills.

Tip 253

I've learned that people will forget what you said, people will forget what you did, but people will never forget how you made them feel.

— Maya Angelou, author, dancer, actress, and singer

Kindness, compassion, and empathy go a long way in creating long-lasting relationships in a new country. Praise and compliments when they are genuine, are such a great way to acknowledge people's efforts.

Tip 254

The difference between a successful person and others is not lack of strength, not a lack of knowledge but rather a lack of will.

— Vince Lombardi, football player, coach, and executive

Almost all economic immigrants are skilled and highly experienced. The only differentiating factor between those who succeed and those who fail is *determination* to pursue their dreams.

Tip 255

I am a simple man. I divide almost everything into two categories. Things I have control over and things I have no control over. Those I have no control over include the weather, global happenings, and how the interviewer or a potential client may feel on a particular day. I do have control over how I react to the weather, the interviewer, the client, or global happenings!

— Nick (Naeem) Noorani, immigrant champion, author, and motivational speaker

Tip 256

Keep your thoughts positive because your thoughts become your words. Keep your words positive because your words become your behavior. Keep your behavior positive because your behavior becomes your habits. Keep your habits positive because your habits become your values. Keep your values positive because your values become your destiny

— Mahatma Gandhi, leader of Indian Independence
Movement, philosopher and peaceful activist

Research indicates that it is one's thoughts that make the difference between success and failure. Negativity saps your energy, leaving you depressed and hopeless. Rather than sitting with friends from your own community and blaming discrimination for not finding a job, you should say, "I am going to develop my language skills to match with those of the natives." Think positive and talk positive.

Tip 257

Only those who will risk going too far can possibly find out how far one can go.

— T.S. Eliot, author, publisher, playwright,
and literary and social critic

There is no limit for success. The more risk you take, the greater the achievements. The world is full of examples of successful and influential immigrants who gave up stable jobs to start their own ventures.

Tip 258

If you are not willing to risk the unusual, you will have to settle for the ordinary.

— Jim Rohn, entrepreneur, author,
and motivational speaker

There is no lack of untapped opportunities in any foreign country, but you must take the risk to mould them into business ventures.

Tip 259

You can measure opportunity with the same yardstick that measures the risk involved. They go together.

— Earl Nightingale, author and motivational speaker

Risk and success are directly proportional — the higher the risk, the greater the success.

Tip 260

All great achievements require time.

— Maya Angelou, author, dancer, actress, and singer

Sometimes we get impatient and want the same level of employment that we had in our home countries. You will get there, but have patience and continuously invest in your own personal and professional development and your efforts will pay off.

Tip 261

Don't be afraid to take a big step. You can't cross a chasm in two small jumps.

— David Lloyd George,
1st Earl Lloyd-George of Dwyfor

The distance to success is not short and simple. Getting a survival job and managing the bills is not the definition of success. You will have to accomplish something extraordinary to make it to the top — maybe exploit a market demand or create one!

Tip 262

The person who risks nothing does nothing, has nothing, is nothing, and becomes nothing. He may avoid suffering and sorrow, but he simply cannot learn and feel and change and grow and love and live.

— Leo F. Buscaglia, author,
motivational speaker, and professor

If you avoid risk, you might live in a safe haven but then you also deprive yourself of new learning and growth.

Tip 263

Great minds discuss ideas, average minds discuss events, small minds discuss people.

— Eleanor Roosevelt, politician and
former first lady of the United States

Demonstrate your intellectual abilities at business meetings and social gatherings by discussing relevant topics. Debate, exchange opinions, and take a genuine interest in what others do or say. Ask questions and listen.

Tip 264

If you talk to a man in a language he understands, that goes to his head. If you talk to him in his own language, that goes to his heart.

— Nelson Mandela, politician, philanthropist,
former President of South Africa, and
anti-apartheid revolutionary

Communication involves learning more than English or French; it involves developing the local language skills — understanding the local phrases and business jargon.

Tip 265

Invest in yourself by taking advanced English classes and business English. Remember, if you don't invest in yourself, why should an employer?

— Nick (Naeem) Noorani, immigrant champion, author, and motivational speaker

Proficiency in the English language is not only a critical factor in finding an appropriate job but also a major determinant of career growth. Invest in business English and other courses to improve your skills.

Tip 266

Did you know that the Chinese symbol for "crisis" includes a symbol which means opportunity?

— Jane Revell, author and trainer; and Susan Norman, author

There are also opportunities hidden in hardships that may provide a chance to learn something new, inspire you to try a different career plan, start your own venture, or build new relationships. Look beyond the problem and seek a solution. I started my magazine in the basement of my house after I was laid off. That was one month after we bought our first house in Canada. Looking back, that crisis made me find a more fulfilling life here.

Tip 267

Volunteering is giving back to get ahead.

— Nick (Naeem) Noorani, immigrant champion, author, and motivational speaker

Volunteer work helps one to gain sufficient experience in a new country and improves access to the job market. It gives opportunities to learn workplace skills and attitudes. You acquire soft skills such as communication skills, knowledge of workplace practices, adapting to and understanding culture, the value of networking, increased self-confidence, and how to work in a diverse workforce.

Tip 268

I'm a great believer in luck, and I find the harder I work the more I have of it.

— Thomas Jefferson, former President of the United States and one of the Founding Fathers of the USA

Though you may have heard people mention someone was successful because he or she was lucky, luck is a by-product of hard work and determination.

Tip 269

The difference between ordinary and extraordinary is that little extra.

— Jimmy Johnson, former football player, coach, and executive

You need to put in that extra effort to realize your dreams. Extra effort means learning new skills, taking risks, meeting new people, and making those tough decisions. Move out of your comfort zone and thrive!

Tip 270

It was a high counsel that I once heard given to a young person, "Always do what you are afraid to do."

— Ralph Waldo Emerson, author and lecturer

Don't be afraid of meeting new people, striking up a conversation, attending events, learning new things, or exploring new possibilities.

Tip 271

Talent hits a target no one else can hit. Genius hits a target no one else can see.

— Arthur Schopenhauer, author and philosopher

I am a huge believer in immigrant genius. For example, one of the co-founders of Google is an immigrant; and eBay was created by an immigrant. We create the limitations in our mind. Think differently!

Tip 272

All of us have within the seeds for greatness. Unless those seeds are nurtured they will not grow!

— Nick (Naeem) Noorani, immigrant champion, author, and motivational speaker

How are you investing in yourself daily? Do you read material relevant to your occupation? Do you study the latest advances in technology? This is the best investment you can make as you climb the staircase of success.

Tip 273

If opportunity doesn't knock, build a door.

— Milton Berle, comedian and actor

We all have to create our own paths to reach our goals. Prospective employers will not come to you to offer you jobs. You will have to earn them through your own initiative.

Tip 274

You need to overcome the tug of people against you as you reach for high goals.

— General George S. Patton, United States army general

Avoid those who try to bring you down either at work or in your personal life. Surround yourself with people who will inspire you to achieve great heights.

Tip 275

You can't expect to hit the jackpot if you don't put a few nickels in the machine.

— Flip Wilson, comedian and actor

You cannot be successful without putting in hard work and investing in yourself.

Tip 276

If you don't make the time to work on creating the life you want, you're eventually going to be forced to spend a lot of time dealing with a life you don't want.

— Kevin Ngo, author

Don't overstay in a survival job. Take some time every day to focus on the areas that will take you closer to your goals.

Tip 277

Today I will do what others won't, so tomorrow I can accomplish what others can't.

— Jerry Rice, former football player

Many immigrants get so comfortable with their survival jobs that they never bother to polish their soft skills which hinder their chances of growth. Avoid this trap and always push yourself to achieve your goals.

Tip 278

The start is what stops most people.

— Don Shula, former football player and coach

Many people fail because they never have the courage to start.

Tip 279

Losers live in the past. Winners learn from the past and enjoy working in the present toward the future.

— Denis Waitley, author, consultant,
and motivational speaker

You should learn from your past mistakes and move on. Develop skills, network with resourceful people, and work hard to gain success in future.

Tip 280

Accept responsibility for your life. Know that it is you who will get you where you want to go, no one else.

— Les Brown, motivational speaker,
former politician, author, and radio DJ

You are responsible for your life. It is in your hand to learn, adapt, and evolve; or stay ignorant and continue being invisible.

Tip 281

If there is a trait which does characterize leaders, it is opportunism. Successful people are very often those who steadfastly refuse to be daunted by disadvantage and have the ability to turn disadvantage to good effect. They are people who seize opportunity and take risks. Leadership then seems to be a matter of personality and character.

— John Viney, author and entrepreneur

Leaders are always resourceful and are never afraid of taking risks. They are willing to learn and upgrade their skills to overcome any failure.

Tip 282

If you limit your choices only to what seems possible or reasonable, you disconnect yourself from what you truly want, and all that is left is a compromise.

— Robert Fritz, author, management consultant, composer, and filmmaker

To achieve success, you must take risks that at times may seem too high. Do not compromise your goals for smaller milestones.

Tip 283

Immigrants need to understand the power of social media — 92 percent of recruiters used LinkedIn, 24 percent [have] hired from Facebook, and 14 percent found their new hires on Twitter. On the flip side, please remember inappropriate social media photos and comments can harm you!

— Nick (Naeem) Noorani, immigrant champion, author, and motivational speaker

Tip 284

Success seems to be connected with action. Successful people keep moving. They make mistakes, but they don't quit.

— Conrad Hilton, entrepreneur and hotelier

You should always be acting on your dreams. That is the only way to move forward and gain success.

Tip 285

The right man is the one who seizes the moment.

— Johann Wolfgang von Goethe, author and statesman

Make the best use of opportunities to showcase your talent, meet new people, and attend social events at work or elsewhere.

Tip 286

There comes a moment when you have to stop revving up the car and shove it into gear.

— David Mahoney, former soccer player

Similarly, your career will advance only when you put your plans and resources into action.

Tip 287

An idea is worthless unless you use it.

— John Maxwell, author, public speaker, and pastor

Your ideas are nothing until you put them into action.

Tip 288

Opportunities don't often come along. So, when they do, you have to grab them.

— Audrey Hepburn, actress and humanitarian

Keep an open and an alert mind. Spot opportunities. I keep a diary by my bedside and write down ideas. The *Canadian Immigrant Magazine* was my 3;00 a.m. dream that changed my life. I also have a folder on my computer titled "Ideas."

Tip 289

Big jobs usually go to the men who prove their ability to outgrow small ones.

— Ralph Waldo Emerson, author and lecturer

Your employer should see your potential to take on more challenging roles and greater responsibilities. Only then will you get career advancement or promotions.

Tip 290

Position yourself as a center of influence, the one who knows the movers and shakers. People will respond to that, and you'll soon become what you project.

— Bob Burg, author and public speaker

Be aware of the powerhouses at your workplace. Being successful in the workplace demands awareness of the politics around you. Understand who you need to influence to achieve results.

Tip 291

Networking is marketing. Marketing yourself, marketing your uniqueness, marketing what you stand for.

— Christine Comaford-Lynch, author

Make yourself and your skills visible to the key people in your workplace — colleagues, supervisors, managers, and leaders. Speak your thoughts, listen to others, and connect outside the office.

Tip 292

Nothing liberates your greatness like the desire to help, the desire to serve.

— Marianne Williamson,
spiritual teacher, author, and lecturer

Get involved in volunteering. It not only gives meaning to life but also a great way to network and acquire work experience in your new country.

Tip 293

God gives every bird his worm, but he does not throw it into the nest.

— Author unknown

Get off that couch now and ask yourself, What can I do today to improve myself?

Tip 294

Initiative is to success what a lighted match is to a candle.

— Orlando Battista, chemist and author

Just like a lighted match ignites a candle, taking initiative to improve your skills and get noticed at the workplace helps you progress toward your goals.

Tip 295

Success depends in a very large measure upon individual initiative and exertion, and cannot be achieved except by a dint of hard work.

— Anna Pavlova, prima ballerina

Success requires effort and a desire to learn new things, adapting to new environments, and exceeding your own expectations.

Tip 296

I don't believe in taking right decisions; I take decisions and then make them right.

— Ratan Tata, businessman and Chairman Emeritus of Tata Sons

Many vacillate before making a decision agonizing over whether it is the right one. Make the decision and make it work.

Tip 297

You look upon the seasons with expectation and await them: way not seize the seasonal opportunities and exploit them?

— Xunzi, Confucian philosopher

Don't wait for time to match your expectations. Grasp the opportunities that come your way and use them to climb up the ladder.

Tip 298

I don't want to get to the end of my life and find that I just lived the length of it. I want to have lived the width of it as well.

— Diane Ackerman, author and naturalist

Don't just live to complete the number of breaths allotted to you. Do something valuable that earns you the respect of generations to come.

Tip 299

An average plan vigorously executed is far better than a brilliant plan on which nothing is done.

— Brian Tracy, entrepreneur, public speaker, author, and personal and professional development trainer

Execution plays a more critical role than planning. Even a brilliant plan can fail without the effort to implement it.

Tip 300

Wear a smile and have friends; wear a scowl and have wrinkles.

— George Eliot, novelist, journalist, and translator

Given how much I smile, I love this tip! Give a friendly smile when you meet colleagues at the workplace or other people you meet in your everyday life. This will help to start friendships.

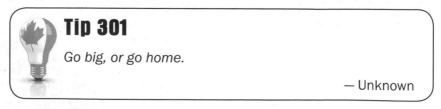

Tip 301

Go big, or go home.

— Unknown

Your decision to come here was driven by the desire to succeed. So why compromise your dreams and settle for less?

Tip 302

Opportunity is missed by most people because it is dressed in overalls and looks like work.

— Thomas Edison, inventor and entrepreneur

Your boss asked you to make a presentation to the senior staff at very short notice. Don't shirk from this duty! Take this as an opportunity to showcase your communication skills, knowledge, confidence, and ability to handle pressure.

Tip 303

My biggest motivation? Just to keep challenging myself. I see life almost like one long University education that I never had — every day I'm learning something new.

— Richard Branson, entrepreneur and investor

My father used to say, the day you stop learning is the day you stop growing. Keep evolving by developing new skills and exploring new opportunities.

Tip 304

A leader is one who knows the way, goes the way, and shows the way.

— John C. Maxwell, pastor, author, and public speaker

Be a leader by setting goals, implementing a plan of action, and setting examples for others to follow.

Tip 305

Leaders think and talk about the solutions. Followers think and talk about the problems.

— Brian Tracy, entrepreneur, public speaker, author, and personal and professional development trainer

Concentrate on finding solutions to problems.

Tip 306

There is a difference between conceit and confidence. Conceit is bragging about yourself. Confidence means you believe you can get the job done.

— Johnny Unitas, former football player

Don't brag about yourself. Show self-confidence through your abilities to complete the job.

Tip 307

Sometimes you have to resist working on your strengths in favor of your weaknesses. The decathlon requires a wide range of skills.

— Daley Thompson, decathlete and Olympic gold medal winner

You may have excellent technical skills but you also need to improve your soft skills to achieve success.

Tip 308

Sometimes we have to go out on a limb and do something different to get noticed.

— Nick (Naeem) Noorani, immigrant champion, author, and motivational speaker

You need to do something different to make yourself visible in your field. Take risks and carve your own path.

Tip 309

People often say that motivation doesn't last. Well, neither does bathing — that's why we recommend it daily.

— Zig Ziglar, author, salesman,
and motivational speaker

Stay motivated to continue. Read a tip every day to fuel the passion.

Tip 310

Good grooming is integral and impeccable style is a must. If you don't look the part, no one will want to give you time or money.

— Daymond John, entrepreneur, investor, television
personality, author, and motivational speaker

Concentrate on improving your appearance and wardrobe to convey confidence and attention to detail.

9

Build Your Self-Confidence

With all the changes and upheaval you have faced so far in your immigration journey, you are bound to have some self-doubt.

You may ask yourself, "Did I make the right decision in bringing my family here? What's wrong with me? Why won't anyone hire me?" We all fall victim to feelings of inadequacy, and question whether we are actually any good at what we do.

Let me tell you a secret: When I first started advising other newcomers, I often questioned whether I had the right to be giving tips on success. After all, I faced plenty of struggle and even today, not everything comes wrapped nicely in a bow. Was I a fraud? One of my mentors gave me this tip: "Fake it until you make it."

Sounds cheeky, perhaps. What I realized is it's talking about self-confidence. Self-confidence comes from the way you speak to yourself. If you're constantly tearing yourself down and telling yourself you're not worthy or good enough, you will lack the confidence to truly take initiative and move forward. If you believe in yourself, then you have the foundation to meet any challenge, even if they are unfamiliar or new at first.

Understand and accept who you are, and the rest will come!

Tip 311

Strive not to be a success, but rather to be of value.

— Albert Einstein, physicist and philosopher of science

Most successful immigrants have chosen a path that adds value to the society as a whole. Evaluate how you can contribute to the host economy. This will open up countless opportunities and accelerate your journey towards success.

Tip 312

Dwell on the beauty of life. Watch the stars, and see yourself running with them.

— Marcus Aurelius, Roman Emperor

Look at the immigrants who have become legends in the history of this new country. Inspire to be among them. If they could do it, why can't you? More importantly, what stops you?

Tip 313

Victorious warriors win first and then go to war, while defeated warriors go to war first and then seek to win.

— Sun Tzu, military general, strategist, and philosopher

Believe in yourself. You have all the capabilities and skills to overcome these challenges. With this confidence go ahead and devise an action plan to overcome the obstacles and emerge a winner.

Tip 314

You are the sum total of everything you've ever seen, heard, eaten, smelled, been told, forgot — it's all there. Everything influences each of us, and because of that I try to make sure that my experiences are positive.

— Maya Angelou, author, dancer, actress, and singer

Be strong. Think strong. Surround yourself with strong, positive people and your life will change.

Tip 315

Risk always brings its own rewards: the exhilaration of breaking through, of getting to the other side; the relief of a conflict healed; the clarity when a paradox dissolves.

— Marilyn Ferguson, author, editor, and public speaker

You have already taken the risk of coming to an unknown land. Now it is time to invest in this effort and reap the benefits. Risk takers are rewarded with success!

Tip 316

Often the difference between a successful man and a failure is not one's better abilities or ideas, but the courage that one has to bet on his idea, to take a calculated risk, and to act.

— Maxwell Maltz, author and cosmetic surgeon

All immigrants are skilled and highly experienced, but what differentiates the highly successful is their self-confidence, ability to take risks, and how they execute their plans with passion and dedication.

Tip 317

The most important thing in communication is hearing what isn't said.

— Peter Drucker, management consultant, educator, and author

Body language reveals a lot more than what you verbally express. Others can read your feelings and thoughts through body posture, gestures, facial expressions, and eye movements. This is especially true during job interviews and business meetings.

Tip 318

I am enough of an artist to draw freely upon my imagination. Imagination is more important than knowledge. Knowledge is limited. Imagination encircles the world.

— Albert Einstein, physicist and philosopher of science

It is important to keep faith in your dreams. Without belief in oneself, no amount of knowledge or technical skills will compensate.

Tip 319

It takes one hour of preparation for each minute of presentation time.

— Wayne Burgraff, philosopher

In a survey conducted, employers said the ability to make presentations is one of the top three qualities they look for in a hire. Good presentation skills are indispensable for a successful career in the corporate world. Look for a Toastmasters event near you to become a better public speaker.

Tip 320

He who wants to persuade should put his trust not in the right argument, but in the right word. The power of sound has always been greater than the power of sense.

— Joseph Conrad, author

Communication skills play an integral role during negotiation and conflict resolution at the workplace.

Tip 321

Believe in yourself! Have faith in your abilities! Without a humble but reasonable confidence in your own powers you cannot be successful or happy.

— Norman Vincent Peale, minister, motivational speaker, and author

Self-confidence and positive thoughts are important to get ahead. Believe in your abilities. Continue to learn and adapt.

Tip 322

If you want to conquer fear, don't sit home and think about it. Go out and get busy.

— Dale Carnegie, author and lecturer

Too much time spent in thinking and planning goes to waste. Conquer your fears by taking action.

Tip 323

When the world says, "Give up"; Hope whispers "Try it one more time."

— Author unknown

You never know how close you were to your goals. Hope keeps your dreams alive. So be optimistic and keep trying until you win.

Tip 324

The greatest mistake you can make in life is to continually fear you will make one.

— Elbert Hubbard, author, publisher, artist, and philosopher

It may not be actually making a mistake that stops you, but the fear of making a mistake. What you fear might turn out to be your greatest asset. Fear is the enemy of action and hope.

Tip 325

Surround yourself with only people who are going to lift you higher.

— Oprah Winfrey, television host, actress, CEO, and author

Build relationships with people who encourage your goals and whose positive attitudes motivate you.

Tip 326

Never tell me the sky's the limit when there are footprints on the moon.

— Author unknown

Success has no limits. As you achieve your existing goals, you can set a new benchmark to reach greater heights. Never stop doing this.

Tip 327

I have been impressed with the urgency of doing. Knowing is not enough; we must apply. Being willing is not enough; we must do.

— Leonardo da Vinci, painter, sculptor, architect, musician, mathematician, engineer, inventor, anatomist, geologist, cartographer, botanist, and author

Apply knowledge gained to solve problems and overcome fears, then you will be able to progress toward your career goals.

Tip 328

Immigrants are natural risk takers and entrepreneurs. You have to be if you give up your security to move to the unknown in another country! Now use this risk-taking ability to your advantage. Many before you have done so to great success. Apply calculated risks to your new life. Learn a new trade. Play a new instrument or take up a sport. Remember the canvas of your life is as big or as small as you want it to be because you are the artist.

— Nick (Naeem) Noorani, immigrant champion, author, and motivational speaker

Tip 329

Example is not the main thing in influencing other people; it's the only thing.

— Abraham Lincoln, former President of the United States

Your actions and body language play an important role in influencing the way others perceive and react to you. Make sure you send a positive message.

Tip 330

Associate yourself with people of good quality, for it is better to be alone than in bad company.

— Booker T. Washington, educator, author, orator, and advisor to the presidents of the United States

Your companions have a great influence on your thoughts. Make friends with those who support your endeavours and avoid those who mock your efforts.

Tip 331

Start every day off with a smile and get it over with.

— W.C. Fields, comedian, actor, juggler, and author

Whatever be the circumstances, start and end your day with a smile. It is a potent weapon to weaken the challenges and strengthen your willpower.

Tip 332

Whatever you can do, or dream you can do, begin it.
Boldness has genius, power, and magic in it.
Begin it now.

— Johann Wolfgang von Goethe, author and statesman

Confidence can overcome any challenge.

Tip 333

Believe in yourself and all that you are. Know that there is something inside you that is greater than any obstacle.

— Christian D. Larson, teacher and author

Have faith in your abilities. You have all the capabilities and strength to overcome any challenge.

Tip 334

Nothing is impossible, the word itself says, "I'm possible"!

— Audrey Hepburn, actress and humanitarian

You will meet several naysayers: people who will try their best to dim your dreams. Stay away from such people and believe in yourself.

10

Be Resilient

It takes resilience to be an immigrant. What is resilience? It is defined as the ability to adapt to stress and adversity, and to persevere through challenges. Having the courage to leave your country, family, friends, culture, and language behind, and adapting to a new life in a foreign land might just be the very definition of resilience.

How are you doing with this? Are you adapting well to the stress of immigrating? Or has your resilience been shaken?

If you're struggling, don't give up. Resilience isn't some static characteristic such as your eye colour or height; it is a state of mind, and it can be built with a positive attitude using the right strategies.

If you reread the last nine chapters, you'll notice that this book is full of the strategies you need to build your resilience. To stay resilient, you need to do the following:

- Understand yourself and your environment.

- Be willing to ask for help.

- Embrace change and focus on positive solutions.

- Take charge of your life and believe in yourself.

- Stay inspired.

These strategies aren't necessarily new — some might even seem obvious — but that doesn't make them any less wise. Often, we just need little reminders to keep us motivated. Hopefully, the wisdom from all the experts I have quoted in this book will keep you inspired as you move forward in your journey in Canada and in life. Any time you falter or face a setback, just pick up this book and reread your favourites!

Tip 335

Two roads diverged in a wood, and I took the one less traveled by, and that has made all the difference.

— Robert Frost, poet

Out-of-the-box thinking and the conviction to tread the more challenging path has been a critical success factor for many immigrants. At times, we miss out on identifying and leveraging the opportunity right in front of us because we prefer safer options rather than taking risks.

Tip 336

If you do what you've always done, you'll get what you've always gotten.

— Tony Robbins, performance coach, author, motivational speaker, and actor

You might have applied to innumerable jobs but with no positive results. If you are not able to get what you want, it's time to change your approach. You may have to undertake classes to improve your language, communication, presentation, and networking skills.

Tip 337

The problem is immigrants give up too soon. We want success, but a lot of us are not willing to pay the price for it.

— Nick (Naeem) Noorani, immigrant champion,
author, and motivational speaker

Many immigrants get quickly disheartened by a series of rejections, no interview call-backs, being overqualified for a position, and biased attitudes, perceived or real, at workplaces. These setbacks cause people to either contemplate leaving the country or compromise their dreams. But don't forget success comes to those who fight back with all their mettle and more. You have to resist, insist, and persist for success!

Tip 338

Just when the caterpillar thought the world was over, she became a butterfly.

— Barbara Haines Howett, author, editor, and journalist

The biggest irony of life is that most miraculous transformations of people happen when they are surrounded by hardships. Unable to find a job that matches your dreams, never-ending financial troubles, growing insecurity, family worries; amidst all this, you can and should reinvent yourself to create a brighter future for you, your family, and your new home!

Tip 339

The true measure of success is how many times you can bounce back from failure.

— Stephen Richards, author

Success is not created overnight. It takes years of effort and hard work to achieve one's dreams. Failure is the only common thing among all the great men and women throughout history.

Tip 340

I will love the light for it shows me the way, yet I will endure the darkness because it shows me the stars.

— Og Mandino, author and public speaker

The known paths always seem to be safe and attractive, but only when you venture into unknown areas can you achieve success.

Tip 341

The time to take counsel of your fears is before you make an important battle decision. That's the time to listen to every fear you can imagine! When you have collected all the facts and fears and made your decision, turn off all your fears and go ahead!

— General George S. Patton,
United States army general

There is no room for fear once you have arrived in your new country. Hopefully you have done all your research and analysis beforehand. Now is the time to work hard, and to make new friends and business associates. Now is the time to execute your plans and do whatever is required to realize your dreams. Now is the time for you to become what you wanted to be — a successful immigrant.

Tip 342

Cherish your visions and your dreams, as they are the children of your soul, the blueprints of your ultimate achievements.

— Napoleon Hill, author, journalist,
salesman, and lecturer

Stay focused on the ultimate goal which prompted you to start a new life in a foreign country. Nurture that goal, and strive for it in every possible way even if it's as simple as a daily affirmation.

Tip 343

I know God won't give me anything I can't handle. I just wish he didn't trust me so much.

— Mother Teresa, nun who founded the Missionaries of Charity

Don't be bogged down by the challenges. You have all the strength and resources to overcome these temporary obstacles to reach your goal.

Tip 344

I can be changed by what happens to me. But I refuse to be reduced by it.

— Maya Angelou, author, dancer, actress, and singer

Adapt to new situations and expectations. Never lose your faith and enthusiasm. Above all, always continue your journey.

Tip 345

An obstacle is often a stepping stone.

— William Prescott, American historian and Hispanist

Obstacles are like stepping stones you must cross to reach your final goal.

Tip 346

If you can't fly then run, if you can't run then walk, if you can't walk then crawl, but whatever you do you have to keep moving forward.

— Martin Luther King, Jr., pastor, activist, humanitarian, and leader of the African-American Civil Rights Movement

Hard work, persistence, and determination are very important for success.

Tip 347

Logic will get you from A to B. Imagination will take you everywhere.

— Albert Einstein, physicist and philosopher of science

Logic and strategy are important, but imagination is the engine that drives creation.

Tip 348

Keep away from people who try to belittle your ambitions. Small people always do that, but the really great make you feel that you, too, can become great.

— Mark Twain, author and humorist

Avoid those who ridicule your dreams. Surround yourself with people who are successful themselves. They will understand your passion to succeed and encourage you to attain your goals.

Tip 349

Everything comes in time to him who knows how to wait.

— Leo Tolstoy, author, philosopher, and political thinker

There is a time for everything. Be patient and continue your efforts. You will eventually get what you aspire for.

Tip 350

The will to win, the desire to succeed, the urge to reach your full potential — these are the keys that will unlock the door to personal excellence.

— Confucius, teacher, politician, and philosopher

Your passion is the fuel for continuing the journey to success. Keep it ignited.

Tip 351

Life's challenges are not supposed to paralyze you, they're supposed to help you discover who you are.

— Bernice Johnson Reagon, singer, composer, scholar, and social activist

Challenges are meant to help you look within and realize your potential to explore hidden opportunities.

Tip 352

Genius is 1 percent inspiration, and 99 percent perspiration.

— Thomas Edison, inventor and entrepreneur

This tip is so simple it really needs no explanation. Having that idea is not enough. It is your own efforts and hard work that have the greatest impact on the results.

Tip 353

For most of us, immigration happens after we have already achieved much in our professions. Immigration is the hardest thing you will ever do. As the years go on it continues to impact our lives. Believe in yourself, resist negativity, and continue investing in yourself.

— Nick (Naeem) Noorani, immigrant champion, author, and motivational speaker

Tip 354

A sense of humor is part of the art of leadership, of getting along with people, of getting things done.

— Dwight D. Eisenhower, former President of the United States and general

A sense of humour is vital for building strong and positive personal and professional relationships.

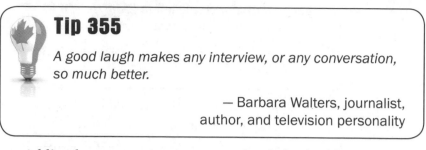

Tip 355

A good laugh makes any interview, or any conversation, so much better.

— Barbara Walters, journalist,
author, and television personality

Adding humour to your conversation helps build rapport with others.

Tip 356

The best measure of happiness is not the size of your wallet, but the size of your smile.

— W. Brett Wilson, entrepreneur, philanthropist,
and panelist on Dragons' Den

True life for a new immigrant can be filled with ups and downs. Sometimes there will be more downs, but the ability to smile will make the journey more bearable. Spend time with positive people and it will be so much easier to smile.

Tip 357

The spirit, the will to win and the will to excel — these are the things that endure and these are the qualities that are so much more important than any of the events that occasion them.

— Vince Lombardi, football player,
coach, and executive

Enthusiasm, determination to win, and an ability to lead others will help you face any challenge.

Tip 358

Smiling a lot can lead to another consequence. Complaining a lot less! Here's an experiment to prove this. Stand in front of the mirror with the biggest smile you can muster and try complaining. You cannot! See? It does work!

— Nick (Naeem) Noorani, immigrant champion, author, and motivational speaker

Tip 359

You are never too old to set another goal or to dream a new dream.

— C.S. Lewis, author, academic, literary critic, and lay theologian

If your Plan A fails, develop another plan to achieve success. It is important to keep moving forward.

Tip 360

Be a yardstick of quality. Some people aren't used to an environment where excellence is expected.

— Steve Jobs, entrepreneur, marketer, and inventor

Make your performance stand out from the crowd and be an inspiration to others to achieve.

Tip 361

You may be disappointed if you fail, but you are doomed if you don't try.

— Beverly Sills, operatic soprano

Keep trying until you achieve what you aspire even if you stumble on the way.

Tip 362

Trust your instincts.

— Estée Lauder, entrepreneur

Listen to both your heart and head while making difficult decisions. Successful leaders rely often on intuition rather than logical thinking.

Tip 363

The greatest glory in living lies not in never falling, but in rising every time we fall.

— Nelson Mandela, former President of South Africa, philanthropist, and anti-apartheid revolutionary

My journey in entrepreneurship was fraught with challenges. On the 17th attempt I was finally successful. The other 16 attempts were lessons in what not to do! However, nothing stopped me from trying until I succeeded.

Tip 364

When we tackle obstacles, we find hidden reserves of courage and resilience we did not know we had. And it is only when we are faced with failure do we realise that these resources were always there within us. We only need to find them and move on with our lives.

— A.P.J. Abdul Kalam, former President of India, scientist, professor, and author

You will go through challenges, but your mind has already forgotten the many challenges you went through years ago when you were just starting your career and how you overcame obstacles small and big. You always scaled greater heights and you can do it again. Believe in yourself and it will happen.

Tip 365

The seeds of greatness are within you.

— Nick (Naeem) Noorani, immigrant champion,
author, and motivational speaker

OTHER TITLES OF INTEREST FROM SELF-COUNSEL PRESS

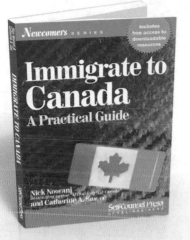

Immigrate to Canada: A Practical Guide

Nick Noorani & Catherine A. Sas, QC

ISBN 978-1-77040-209-6

6 x 9 • paper • 184 pp.

First Edition: October 2014

$21.95 USD/CAD

Canada is one of the world's most welcoming countries, a relatively new land built by immigration with some of the top cities in which to live. But how do you turn your dreams abroad into reality in Canada? This book, part of the *Newcomers* series, gives you the critical advantage in understanding how to prepare to come to Canada. It shows you how to navigate the government maze and how to ensure your paperwork is in order. And it provides insights from its experienced authors on what to expect on your journey.

The Authors

Nick Noorani is a social entrepreneur, immigration champion and motivational speaker. He was the founding publisher of Canadian Immigrant magazine and wrote the federal government's guide to immigration for newcomers, among other publications. Nick is a well-known authority on improving immigrant outcomes. He has become a powerful voice for the successful integration of immigrants in Canada and bridging cultural gaps in the workplace and beyond.

Catherine A. Sas, QC, is a leading immigration lawyer based in Vancouver and a Partner in the Immigration group. With over 20 years of experience, she provides a full range of immigration services and has been recognized as a leading immigration practitioner by Lexpert, Who's Who Legal, and Best Lawyers in Canada.